Countries In The Bible: Who They Are Today

Flying Eagle Publications

We aspire to create materials that encourage and strengthen you in your journey through life. It is also our aim to equip believers so that they can reach farther dream larger and get their message heard. The eagle flies closest to the Creator and bears His message to all. That is our hope too. That is why we do what we do– to teach, entertain and inspire.

Countries In The Bible:

Who They Are Today

Flying Eagle Publications
flyingeaglepublications.com

Unless otherwise noted, all scripture taken from the King James Version of the Bible. Scriptures marked KJV are taken from the KING JAMES VERSION (KJV): KING JAMES VERSION, public domain.

Scriptures marked ASV are taken from the American Standard Version (ASV); American Standard Version, public domain.

Illustrations: Haley Jula
Cover image by Mariam Soliman courtesy of Unsplash.

Countries In The Bible: Who They Are Today
Print ISBN: 978-0-9766268-4-8

Copyright © 2018 Flying Eagle Publications
All Rights Reserved under International Copyright Law. No part of this book may be reproduced or transmitted in any form or by any means without written permission of the publisher. Flyingeaglepublications.com

Printed in the United States.

Table of Contents

Countries in the Bible..9

Israel..29

Palestine..47

Islamic Terrorism...63

Prophecies About the Middle East...................................79

Bibliography...107

-This little book is heavy with information. We don't apologize for that. Proceed slowly; breathe. Use the first and last chapters like a reference tome if you desire. Come back to it as often as needed. You are enlarging your store of knowledge and feeding your mind. Enjoy the process.

♣ The Editors

• Chapter 1 •

Countries in the Bible

Did you know that most of the Middle East is really Western Asia? The region has many foods such as lamb, dates, figs, raisins, pita bread, phyllo (fie lo), lentils and eggplants common in their cooking traditions. But the area is a melting pot of ancient people groups. Archaeology has helped us understand these groups, and the history reveals that what the Bible says about these cultures is correct.

Many of the people groups and their civilizations mentioned in the Bible were unknown to us. Since no records of them were found anywhere else, the information the Bible provided was thought to be myth and legend. That theory has been proven wrong over and over by each ancient discovery.

Genesis 10 lists the descendants of Noah's sons, Ham, Shem and Japheth. These three sons represent three groups all ethnologists agree on: African, Asian, European. Ethnology is a science that studies the origin and movement of cultures and analyzes, compares and divides people into groups according to their similarities or differences. Ethnologists do their best to separate man into races and define their culture.

The list in Genesis is called the Table of Nations. The names listed consist of seventy nations from which all nations on earth are derived. From these people and the three areas represented by Noah's sons, Ham/Africa, Shem/Asia, Japheth/Europe, our modern world has developed and is ever changing as man moves, mingles and settles.

A fifteen year old Israeli youth had a vision for the future of Israel.[1] He said that seventy nations were about to come against them. Perhaps from God's perspective seventy nations makes up the *all the earth* reference in Zechariah 12:3. "And in that day will I make Jerusalem a burdensome stone for all people: all that burden themselves with it shall be cut in pieces, though all the people of the earth be gathered together against it."

The seventy nations have been observed by Israel before. When former Israeli President Shimon Perez died September 2016, leaders from seventy nations came to pay their respect. In January 2017, leaders from seventy nations met in Paris to condemn Israel's right to the land of Israel. Rabbi Trugman said in an interview with *Breaking Israel News* "What's interesting is that it isn't just one or two enemies with a specific grudge, like the Arabs or the Nazis. It is 70 nations, which in Torah terms, means all of the nations." The Torah is the first five books of the Old Testament. The Jewish rabbis take their interpretation of these events not only from Genesis 10 but Numbers also.

"There is no doubt this is a fulfillment of the prophecies that in the end of days, all the nations will come out against Israel," the rabbi

---

[1] You can listen to the young man's story at https://www.youtube.com/watch?v=fe08-NUTqTc. Keep in mind that this boy's experience is a secular Jew's encounter with heaven and not told from a Christian perspective.

added.[2] So, one of the end time prophecies for the Middle East may already be in progress.

The area we know today as the Middle East is divided into countries with permanent boundaries. Many of these boundaries were chosen in the 20th century (1900s) after the Ottoman Empire collapsed during World War I. The Ottoman Turks (from Turkey) had ruled the region since 1299. Their first ruler was Osman I. Othmān is the Arabic version of his name and was the origin of Ottoman. The Ottomans were Muslims, and they were in power until 1922.

Following World War I, the area was controlled by European countries, England, France, Russia and Italy. Maps were drawn, boundaries were made and countries were created. Oil was first discovered in Iran in 1903. In 1938 it was discovered in Saudi Arabia. This interested the Europeans and Americans. One by one, however, individual countries gained their independence as the European foreign powers withdrew after World War II. (Cyprus was the last to gain its independence from Britain in 1960.)

But in ancient times, the dividing lines were more fluid. Boundaries depended on agreements with neighboring kings or tribal chieftains. The agreements were always subject to raids and wars.

The most common government in the region was a city-state system. Each city had a king who ruled and defended smaller neighboring towns and outlying districts. There were also nomad tribes of the desert who organized themselves by family and clan and ruled their territories.

Some city-states were walled for protection against raids and wars. Some were not as in the case of the Perizzite communities. The Perizz-

---

[2] Facts and quotes from "Biblical Origins of the 70-Nation Anti-Israel Paris Conference" By Adam Eliyahu Berkowitz January 5, 2017, *Breaking Israel News*.

ites were a people group whose name refers to open country. According to *Fausset's Bible Dictionary*, the Hebrew word *perezot* means unwalled country villages. The word unwalled may imply villages of farming communities like what we see in rural areas today.

The people of the Middle East were a mix of descendants belonging to Ham, Shem and Japheth, Noah's sons. The people intermarried and built cities or farmed, kept flocks and hunted. They spread throughout the area. The list in Genesis 10 includes where the people settled and the origins of people groups such as Europeans, Asians, Cretes/Greeks, Persians, etc.

The area lying along the Mediterranean was called Canaan and settled by Ham's and Shem's descendants. This was the land God promised to give Abraham through his son Isaac. Much of Canaan and what the Bible calls Arabia was later taken over by the descendants of Abraham's other sons.

Abraham is an important figure because he was born around 1950 BC in Mesopotamia and traveled through what is today Turkey, Syria, Jordan, Israel and Egypt. The account of his life has enlightened historians and been supported by archaeological discoveries. But he is also famous for being the father of two cultures and two major religions.

The area he traveled is what historians call Mesopotamia, but he knew it by local names like *Beth Nahrain*, The Land of Rivers, tribal names, and by the empires of his day. Let's begin in Iraq and follow Abraham's travels for a brief history of the countries as we know them today.

Iraq

Ur was an important trade city in the Sumerian Empire, located near where the Tigris and Euphrates Rivers flow into the Persian Gulf.

Abraham is said to have lived there during the height of its wealth and culture. King Belshazzar's name was discovered inscribed near a pagan temple in Ur. Scholars did not think he was the king at the time the Persians invaded.

Iraq is also associated with the ancient land of Babylon. Babylon means gate of the gods. The city of Babylon was built by Nimrod, a descendant of Ham. Nimrod lived before Abraham. Some scholars connect Nimrod with Sargon of Akkad mentioned in ancient texts. Whether he is Sargon or not is interesting, but it is not the main issue in the Bible. Babylon is said to be the birthplace of an anti-God message that promoted worship of the sun, moon and stars. Babylon is the source for all pagan religions and their ideas.

Babylon is famous for the Tower of Babel, a ziggurat type structure. Babel means confused. Some archaeologists are looking at Tel Brak in Syria as the location of the Tower. Others think they have uncovered its foundation in Babylon. The area of Iraq was also called the land of Shinar which included what is today northwest Syria.

Iraq was the center of the Sumerian and Babylonian Empires, Old and New. It was the location of the Hanging Gardens, one of the Seven Wonders of the Ancient World. Supposedly, King Nebuchadnezzar had the gardens built for his wife who was homesick for her lush green country in northwest Iran.

Nebuchadnezzar is mentioned in the Bible many times, especially in the book of Daniel. Berlin's Pergamum Museum has reconstructed another of Nebuchadnezzar's wonders, the Ishtar Gate. It was the main gate into the city and honored the goddess, Ishtar.

Ezekiel was taken to Babylon. His tomb is there. Daniel was also taken to Babylon. Both men had visions of end time events while living in Iraq.

Other important Empires and people groups overlapped Iraq's boundaries in ancient history. The Hittites, Hurrians, Mitanni and Assyrians were neighbors. Assyria was called the land of Nimrod in Micah 5:6. Nuzi was an important city in the Hurrian Empire which included the Horites, Jebusites and Hivites. At Khorsabad archaeologists discovered Sargon's fortress. Many skeptics thought he was a mythical king. Calah, Tell al-Rimah and Bagdad are also important cities. Many artifacts were destroyed in the Iraq War.

The Tigris and Euphrates are major rivers in the area. These may not be the original rivers associated with the Garden of Eden but could be renamed for them. Nineveh was the capital of the Assyrian Empire. The prophet Jonah, visited Nineveh which is today Mosul. Much of Mosul was destroyed by ISIS forces in 2014. The city of Babylon is near al-Hillah, fifty miles south of Baghdad. Ur is about 10 miles south of Nasiriyah.

Turkey

Turkey is the region of Gog, Lud and Gomer in the Old Testament. Gomer is also linked to Germany because Gomer had a son named Ashkenaz whose descendants traveled into Europe. (Genesis 10:3) Turkey overlapped with part of what is the country of Armenia today. It is also associated with Gog, Togarmah, Tubal and Meshech in Ezekiel 38 which includes the rest of Armenia and its neighbor, Azerbaijan. Meshech is thought to be Moscow.

The Ararat Mountain Range is in Turkey. Somewhere in these mountains Noah's ark came to rest. It is from this area many believe civilizations began to develop.

A *National Geographic* article by Andrew Curry describes the

Göbekli Temple. It is a discovery that has upset the evolutionary theory of civilization's chain of events. This theory says that man has progressed from hunter-gatherers to farmers and then to builders of cities over a long period of time.

But the temple predates their timeline, putting civilization, or town building, at the time when people were supposed to be farming. There are other temple cities nearby. Clearly man was building cities very early in his history.

Abraham traveled to the city of Haran in southern Turkey. You might confuse the name of this town with the name of Abraham's brother. The English spelling of the town is the same as Abraham's brother, Haran. But the town is Charan (H2771 *Strong's*) and means parched, and Abraham's brother's name Haran means mountaineer.

Large ancient empires ruled in this region, including the Lydians, Hittites and the Assyrians. The Hittites and the Assyrians are mentioned many times in the Old Testament. The Hittites were a powerful empire with iron chariots. They were also expert horsemen and perhaps the first terrorists. 2Kings 7 records the fact that just the thought of Hittites sent the Syrian army running. The ancient Hittite capitol is near modern day Boğazkale east of Ankara.

The Assyrians also struck terror into the hearts of those in their path. Many towns surrendered instead of experiencing horrific tortures and brutal deaths. The Assyrian Royal Court Records support the Bible's description of them. Assyrian armies threatened Israel's kings several times. A miraculous encounter is recorded in 2Kings 18, 2Chronicles 32, and Isaiah 36-37. Both the Assyrians and the Hittites fought for and against Egypt at different times in their histories.

The land of Turkey had an important role in spreading Christianity. Paul was born in Tarsus in eastern Turkey. Timothy lived in Lystra.

Paul traveled in Turkey during his missionary journeys. These are some of the towns or districts of this area mentioned in the Bible: Ephesus, Colassae, Galatia, Troas, Pergamum (Bergama today), Laodicea, Sardis, Philadelphia, Cappadocia and Antioch (Antakya).

It was in Antioch that believers were first called Christians. Do you see a few New Testament books represented by these names? The books were letters written to believers in these regions. Turkey has many biblical sites, and plays a large role in endtime events.

Syria

Syria is Aram in the Bible, the same name as one of Shem's sons. Aram is a Semitic word that means high table land. It included the northern area between the Tigris and Euphrates. Balaam lived in the hills of Syria. The people are called Arameans. Don't confuse this word with the country of Armenia.

According to the *World Atlas*, Damascus, Syria's capital, is one of the oldest continually inhabited cities in the world. It has been destroyed by wars and rebuilt several times. Padan-aram is another name identified with Syria in the Bible.

Abraham's brother Nahor lived in northeastern Syria. Abraham's son, Isaac, married a woman named Rebekah from this region. Abraham's grandson Jacob also married women from Syria. Jacob first married Leah and then Rachel. Jacob lived in the area until he returned to his father's homeland in present day Israel.

Hittites and Phoenicians were present in Syria as well as Amorites. Ebla was a major kingdom in Syria and an important center for trade. Excavations have supported the biblical narrative of the region. Syria was under the rule of the Babylonian, Assyrian and Persian Empires.

In the Old Testament, the Israelite tribe of Manasseh had land in Syria. Joshua and David went to war with Syrian kings. Solomon's kingdom reached into southern Syria. In the New Testament, Jesus spoke Aramaic. He traveled in Syria and healed a woman's daughter there. Matthew 4:24 says, "And his [Jesus] fame went throughout all Syria."

Lebanon

Lebanon is a country of mountains, cedars and sparkling water. Its beauty inspired Solomon and the Psalmists to write about it. Lebanon is mentioned in the Bible over seventy times. It has also been called Phoenicia and Greater Syria. It was also called Senir or Sion, the home of the Sidonians and connected with Mt. Hermon. Sidon is one of Canaan's sons listed in Genesis 10.

The Sidonians fought alongside the Amalekites against Israel (Judges 10:12). The tribes of Naphtali and Asher had land in southern Lebanon. It was near the town of Tyre that Elijah raised the widow's son from the dead. Solomon used Lebanon's cedars to build the Temple in Jerusalem. Jezebel lived in Sidon (also spelled Zidon). Jesus visited Tyre and Sidon, and Paul visited there in Acts 21:3-7. He sailed from Sidon to Rome. (Acts 27:3) Lebanon was an important stronghold for Christianity into the 1900s.

Jordan

Bible History Daily calls Jordan the other Biblical Land. It was included in the original plans for the nation of Israel. Rabbath Ammon was its capitol in the Bible or just Rabbah. Uriah the Hittite, one of David's Mighty Men, died near Rabbah. (2Samuel 11).

Jordan was the region where Abraham's neighbors lived, and he engaged in a war with some of them in Genesis 14. He won the battle and rescued his nephew Lot from among the hostages.

The cities of Sodom and Gomorrah (Genesis 18-19) were located in Jordan, and Jordan was the area where Lot's sons, Ammon and Moab, settled.

Ammon's family became the Ammonites. They were allies of the Syrians and enemies of Israel. Moab's family became the Moabites and settled south of the Ammonites near the center of the region along the east side of the Dead Sea.

The Moabites raided Hebrew territory. One of their kings, Eglon, is described as extremely fat in Judges 3:17 and another, Mesha, offered his child as a burnt offering during a battle. Another king named Balak hired Balaam the Syrian to curse Israel so they would be destroyed.

Nehemiah recorded that the Moabites were working against him to rebuild the Temple. Moab proved to be Israel's enemy throughout the Old Testament. Not surprisingly, Israel's prophets foretold their doom and destruction. The only honorable Moabite mentioned was Ruth who was among Jesus' ancestors. Her story is found in the book of Ruth.

The Edomites lived in southern Jordan. The Edomites were Esau's descendants. David fought them, and Israel's kings continued to fight them until Israel ceased being a country. All of these groups in Jordan were Israel's cousins, and all were sworn enemies of Israel.

It was in Jordan that Moses climbed Mt. Nebo to see the Promised Land. Mt. Nebo is located near the town of Madaba. Today if you visit Mt. Nebo, it is possible to see the Jordan River, the West Bank (Judea and Samaria), Jerusalem and the Dead Sea.

Petra is an important archaeological site today, and it is in this area that Aaron might have been buried. A people called Nabataeans carved beautiful temples into the rocks there at least three hundred years before Jesus was born.

John the Baptist's ministry was in Jordan. Jesus was baptized in the Jordan River and may have traveled through Jordan on His way to Jerusalem. Jordan's capital, Amman, is fifty miles from Jerusalem. Matthew 4:25 reads, "And there followed him great multitudes from Galilee and Decapolis and Jerusalem and Judaea and from beyond the Jordan." (ASV)

Egypt

Misraim was a son of Ham. Egypt is known as Mizraim or *Misr* today. Egypt's name has remained the same throughout history. It is where Abraham and others went when there was a famine.

Abraham's great grandson, Joseph, became the vizier of Egypt. A vizier was an official second in command directly under the pharaoh. Egypt is where the Israelites were made slaves, Moses was born, the slaves were freed, and where God showed His might to Pharaoh. At times, Egypt helped other empires fight against their enemies. It is where Joseph and Mary took baby Jesus until King Herod died. (Matthew 2:20)

Greece

Greece is represented in the Old Testament by Javan, a son of Japheth. Daniel predicted the rise and fall of the Greek Empire. Kittim is Cyprus. Crete is a name we recognize, and it too is used in the Bible along with Macedonia. The Phoenicians were of Greek descent who settled along the western shore of the Mediterranean in Lebanon.

Caphtor is mentioned too, and while some think this region was really Crete, the Bible lists Caphtor as descending from Casluhim which is thought to be an area between ancient Egypt and Canaan (modern Israel). Likewise the Philistines are thought to be transplants from Crete, but the Bible says they came from Caphtor and were what was left of Caphtor. (Deut. 2:23; Jeremiah 47:4; Amos 9:7) The Philistines are also said to be descended from the Casluhim in Genesis 10:14. The Philistines' identity is still debated by archaeologists, but wherever they lived and migrated from, we can be confident they are relatives of the Egyptians and descendants of Ham.

In the New Testament, there are many mentions of Greece, its culture as practiced by the Roman Empire and influence evident throughout the Middle East.

Libya

Abraham did not visit Libya or Ethiopia. Put was a son of Ham and brother of Misraim. Put or Phut was the ancient name for the region known today as Libya and Algeria, perhaps Tunisia and a portion of Yemen. It is mentioned in the Bible for its dealings with Egypt. The city of Cyrene, listed in the New Testament, is modern day Tripoli. That means that the Simon of Cyrene who carried Jesus' cross lived in Tripoli. Also an evangelist named Lucius (Acts 13:1) was from Cyrene. Put provided soldiers for Egypt's armies.

Ethiopia

Cush was another of Ham's sons. Part of Cush's family settled in Ethiopia while others traveled into Arabia. Cush's family, Nimrod and others, also built the city and culture of Babylon in Iraq. But, Cush, when mentioned as a country in the Bible, usually means Ethiopia. It was also allied with Egypt and provided soldiers for its armies.

In Acts 8, Philip encounters an official of the Ethiopian queen Candace. Cush had many female rulers who are depicted as warrior queens. The Cushite kingdom included part of Sudan and was also called Nubia.

Saudi Arabia

Genesis 16 says Abraham lived between Shur and Kadesh west of Arabia, and he probably never traveled all of Arabia or Yemen.

Arabia, Kedar, Dedan and Midian were located in modern day Saudi Arabia. Saudi Arabia is the region where Abraham's son, Ishmael, settled and those listed in Genesis 25:1-2, "Abraham married Keturah, and they had six sons: Zimran, Jokshan, Medan, Midian, Ishbak, and Shuah."

The text is clear that Abraham sent them away from his son Isaac and that he sent them east. "And Abraham gave all that he had unto Isaac. But unto the sons of the concubines, which Abraham had, Abraham gave gifts, and sent them away from Isaac his son, while he yet lived, eastward, unto the east country." (Genesis 25:5-6)

These sons were the step family of the Hebrews. Esau, however, a Hebrew by birth, also settled in this area. His family became the Edomites, and their territory flowed north into modern day Jordan and south into Saudi Arabia.

Abraham's sons and grandsons from Hagar and Keturah mixed with the Edomites on their border. There were other people in the region too, those not related directly to Abraham and descended from various other sons of Shem and some even from Ham and Japheth all mixed together. These groups became the Arabian nations. Abraham's sons fought with the Horites, a people who lived in caves, and other Canaanite tribes settled nearby.

Ishmael's land stretched from Shur to Havilah in the east. This is thought to be located in a line running through present day Saudi Arabia, originating in ancient Midian and ending in the western edge of southern Iraq. It would have included modern day Kuwait and the countries in the Arabian Peninsula. The thing to note is that it was east of Abraham and Isaac.

In the Bible Arabia is also referred to as Kedar, one of Ishmael's sons (Ezekiel 27:21, Jeremiah 49:28). Dedan is another name for a region in Arabia and also a grandson of Abraham.

Moses fled to Midian (also Abraham's son's name) after killing an Egyptian. He married a Midianite woman and lived there for forty years. Midian was located in Arabia bordering the Red Sea and the Sinai Peninsula. The real mountain of Moses is thought to be in this region. The Hebrew slaves wandered in Arabia. Elijah probably came to Arabia when he fled from Jezebel.

Debates continue whether or not the Wilderness of Shur and Paran were in this region. It is known that Solomon used the port city of Ezion-geber to build his ships. So did Jehoshaphat. Paul went to Arabia after he met Jesus on the road to Damascus, Syria. (Galatians 1).

Yemen

Yemen is the ancient country of Sheba. Sheba is the name of one of Cush's grandsons (Genesis 10:28) and one of Abraham's (Genesis 25:3). The Queen of Sheba sailed to see Solomon. An ancient historian named Josephus calls her the Queen of Egypt and Ethiopia. Jesus called her the Queen of the South. Ezekiel 27:22 refers to Sheba's merchants and their rich spices, gems and gold. They are also called Sabaeans.

Some of Dedan's family also settled in this region. Ophir is another name associated with the southern reaches of the Arabian Peninsula.

Yemen was the center of the kingdom of Himyar, a Jewish/Christian empire, 100-600AD. Himyar was an important power, controlling parts of Saudi Arabia including Yathrib which Muhammad renamed Medina.

Iran

Iran is ancient Persia. It is called Elam, a son of Shem. Cherdorlaomer was one of Persia's early kings. He took hostages in a battle, and Lot, Abraham's nephew, happened to be one of them (Genesis 14). Iran was also called the land of the Medes and the Persians.

It is significant that it is the only country other than Israel that God calls chosen. It is also the only other nation, again besides Israel, out of which God said He would bring a Messiah.

God had a special purpose for Persia. Isaiah 45 describes a man called Cyrus. Isaiah spoke his prophecy 150 years before Cyrus was born. Daniel, as a captive in Babylon, foresaw Cyrus' takeover of the Babylonian Empire.

When Cyrus became the leader of the Babylonians, he came into contact with Daniel and the Hebrew captives. Cyrus is remembered for creating a new policy for kings conquering empires. His policy allowed captives under former leaders to return to their native lands. It respected the captives' gods and helped to rebuild their cities. This policy strengthened his rule because it made the former prisoners happy and loyal followers.

In Persia, Hebrews were favored. One example is Daniel 6:28. Ezra and Nehemiah give the account of Cyrus helping to rebuild the Jewish Temple. The Cyrus Cylinder in the British Museum supports the Bible's history and prophecies about ancient Persia. The book of Esther takes place in Iran during a threat against the Jews as a people. Esther, a Hebrew, was King Xerxes' wife. Xerxes is well documented in history. Parthian is another name associated with a later Persian Empire.

Jews remained influential in Persia. Most scholars believe that the wise men in the story of Jesus' birth came from Persia. The government of modern day Iran is an enemy of Israel. Many Iranians, however, are secretly converting to Christianity.

These are the countries of the Middle East in the Bible. We will take a look at Israel in a separate chapter.

All these countries were polytheistic, meaning that they worshipped many gods. They worshiped false gods named Baal, Chemosh, Marduke, Ashteroth, Molech, Ra and many, many others. They had separate languages but the people were related, some more distantly than others.

There were differences in culture north to south and east to west. But there were many things common to them like food, methods of travel and styles of clothing. Living together in mountains, deserts, coastal lands and plains were nomads, city dwellers, wine-makers, farmers, shepherds and even cave dwellers. It still exists today in some of the same measure.

All of these nations became enemies of Israel. Starting in Ezekiel 25, Ezekiel proclaims God's judgment against these nations due to their various reasons for gloating over Israel's demise. The identity of these countries has not been lost. God has always known them, and we can too.

Acts 2:1-12 tells the account of how men were filled with the Holy Spirit at Pentecost. Acts 2:8-11says, "And how hear we every man in our own tongue, wherein we were born? Parthians, and Medes, and Elamites, and the dwellers in Mesopotamia, and in Judaea, and Cappadocia, in Pontus, and Asia, Phrygia, and Pamphylia, in Egypt, and in the parts of Libya about Cyrene, and strangers of Rome, Jews and proselytes, Cretes and Arabians, we do hear them speak in our tongues the wonderful works of God."

Did you hear all those people groups? All the places of the Middle East are represented. Jews had been scattered over the region by conquering empires. Some were converts to the Jewish religion from those areas where they came in contact with the Hebrews.

God knew the identities of the people living in these countries. He cared for them and provided for them even though they worshipped other gods. Sometimes the wickedness grew to a point that God could no longer ignore it. But after Jesus' resurrection, in love, He provided them a chance to hear the Good News of Jesus.

Empires rose and fell. People moved about. But God had His people in every land, ready to take what they saw and heard of this Jesus back home with them. Christian Iranians would take the message to China. Many of the countries had thriving Christian communities at the time of Muhammad. (Before Mosul was destroyed by ISIS in the summer of 2014, it had Christians whose descendants dated back to the time of Jonah.)

Today God's invitation still stands to the people of the Middle East. Jesus' work on the cross is finished so that anyone who wants to can have the grace and mercy God provided. God's desire is for the nations to accept Him. The Kingdom is at hand, Jesus said. Now the door is wide open.

Gray shaded area: region of Gog and Magog

Israel's current boundaries

• Chapter 2 •

Israel

Israel is 1/10 of 1% of the land in the Middle East. Eight million people live in an area the size of New Jersey. You can drive the length of Israel, north to south, in seven hours. You can cross its narrowest point in about twenty minutes. Israel is not a big country, but it is the center of the Middle East.

It is a young country. Modern Israel is only seventy years old. And, for such a small, young country, it has accomplished a lot. For example, it has the fourth largest air force in the world; it is one of eight countries to send a satellite into space; Israel invented cell phone technology, USB drives, hands free computers, instant messaging, solar windows and cherry tomatoes. It is a leader in ag technology and created unmanned flight. It invented technology to prevent traffic accidents and the Pill Cam, a device you swallow instead of having a colonoscopy. It is the only country in the Middle East where women have equal rights, and it is the Middle East's only democracy.

That's not even a complete list.

Israel is a country of surprises. But the biggest surprise is that it even exists today. The history of Israel and its relationship with God forms most of the Bible. It is through Israel that we see God's desire for the world. The story begins with a man and a journey.

You may know the man was Abraham and his son's name was Isaac. You many know Isaac's descendants became the nation of Israel. But Abraham knew none of these things in the beginning. He did know his name wasn't Abraham. His name was Abram. Later, God added two letters to his name that changed his life.

But why would God choose Abram and then change his name? Those are questions we will be able to answer by the end of this chapter. For now let's begin in the beginning which takes us to Genesis 11:26.

Abram was born around 1950 BC and lived in Ur, an important, prosperous city at the time. *Bible History Online* says that "the history in this region exceeds that of Egypt and its pyramids." There were two main living conditions in Ur, the common and the religious. But even the common had schools, libraries, nice homes and stores.

Abram had two brothers, Nahor and Haran. His father's name was Terah. His brother Haran had two daughters and a son named Lot, but Haran died. They were descendants of Shem through his son Arphaxad and his grandson Eber. Eber is said to be the father of the Hebrews. His brother Joktan had sons whose names appear in Arabia. (Genesis 10:25-29)

Abram moved with his wife, his father and his nephew Lot to Charan in Turkey. When he was seventy-five, God spoke to him and told him to go to the land of Canaan.

Genesis 12:1-3 records the promise God made to him:

> Now the LORD had said unto Abram, Get thee out of thy country, and from thy kindred, and from thy father's house, unto a land that I will shew thee: And I will make of thee a great nation, and I will bless thee, and make thy name great; and thou shalt be a

blessing: And I will bless them that bless thee, and curse him that curseth thee: and in thee shall all families of the earth be blessed.

This may have been the second time God spoke to him about it, the first in Ur which prompted his move to Charan. However it happened, God wanted him to keep moving.

Notice that it was a promise that required action. It was a wonderful promise. But he would have to leave all his family and friends and put his trust in God. This promise came to be called the covenant. A covenant is like a legal contract between two parties, the two parties here being God and Abram.

If you've read Genesis, you might have noticed that Abram didn't leave all his family behind. Lot and his father were with him. Terah died in Charan, but Lot did indeed go along to Canaan and proved to be a problem for Abram later. You might have also noticed that Abram and his wife didn't have any children. Abram obeyed God about moving to Canaan, and they traveled throughout the land, camping out for a while then moving on. Abram called himself a stranger and a visitor in Genesis 23:4.

God revealed more details of this covenant as time went on. In Genesis 15, Abram learns that he will have a son in his old age. This son would multiply into so many descendants that they would be like the stars in the sky. God also said they would be afflicted and even enslaved for a time in the future, but He would deliver them and bring them back to the land Abram was traveling.

Then, God laid out Abram's territory. It includes some big names like the Hittites. "Unto thy seed have I given this land, from the river of Egypt unto the great river, the river Euphrates: The Kenites, and the Kenizzites, and the Kadmonites, And the Hittites, and the Perizzites, and the Rephaims, And the Amorites, and the Canaanites, and the Girgashites, and the Jebusites. (Genesis 15:18 -21)

A long time passed and no son arrived. Abram's wife invented a solution. It was not a good one. She gave Abram an Egyptian slave woman as a second wife so he could have a son. This woman was Hagar. Abram was eighty-five when he made the decision to have a child with another woman. The Bible says he listened to his wife. He should have asked God if this was the right plan. He would have found out it wasn't. Abram was eighty-six when Hagar's son, Ishmael, was born. God did not speak to him for thirteen years. It was a time full of family strife.

Then in Genesis 17, God tells Abram that He desired a relationship between them, a walk based on purity in honoring God. "I am the Almighty God; walk before me, and be thou perfect. And I will make my covenant between me and thee, and will multiply thee exceedingly." (Genesis 17:1-2)

If Abram wanted to be loyal to Him, to do exactly as he was told, he would be greatly blessed. Then, God changed Abram's name from high father to father of a multitude of nations, Abraham.

Abram was respected. He was wise. Surely those in his household honored him, and his neighbors had to admit he was blessed and really rich. Abram didn't have any problems seeing this in his life. What he had trouble imagining was having a child with his wife who had never become pregnant, and now she was eighty-nine and he was ninety-nine!

Did you ever read Romans 4:17? "God... calleth those things which be not as though they were." It means God talks about something as if it has already happened. This verse is about Abram. When God changed his name, Abraham hoped. Hope is like a vision in your head. It helped Abraham to picture himself as God saw him, the father of many nations, and he believed the word God had spoken to him. Then, he started introducing himself as Abraham.

Can you imagine the raised eyebrows? An old man with one kid whose mother was a slave girl calling himself the father of multitudes? If they did snicker, they didn't snicker for long. Starting at 100 years old, Abraham would eventually have seven more sons, the oldest being the promised son Isaac.

During this encounter with God, Abraham also received the instructions to circumcise all males born in his household, Hebrew or foreigner. Males only. God never asked for females of any age to be circumcised.

God extended this agreement which included the rite of circumcision to all of Abraham's descendants. Even in the future, any man who wanted to be included in God's covenant with Abraham had to be circumcised. God also revealed that kings would arise from his family. This meant they would not be visitors as Abraham was in Canaan; they would be the rulers of the land. And, even though God would bless Ishmael, the son of the slave woman, he was not the son God was making this agreement with. Eventually, Abraham sent Hagar and Ishmael away.

In Genesis 18, God told Abraham it was time for this promised child to be born. So, at a hundred years old, his wife Sarah was ninety, Abraham had a son and they were all laughing…in joy. Just think about your elderly grandparents having a baby. That would be news, wouldn't it?

It is important to realize that the covenant agreement was between God, Abraham and Sarah, their son Isaac and his descendants.

It is important to know who was not included in the promise: Ishmael, the six other sons of Abraham with his second wife Keturah:

Zimran, Jokshan, Medan, Midian, Ishbak, and Shuah, their descendants and all the other people living in the region.

What the agreement meant was God was going to take the land away from the Canaanites and give it to Abraham and Sarah's son Isaac and his descendants. Isaac had a son named Jacob whom God called Israel. Jacob had twelve sons, and their families became the Israelites and later the nation of Israel. The rest of the blessings would also belong to them.

Does it sound unfair that God would take land away from one people and give it to another? Have you ever wondered why God would give the Israelites the Canaanites' land?

To answer those questions, we need to understand the purpose for Abraham's journey and the requirements for that purpose to be fulfilled. He was to separate himself from his own nation and set himself apart to God. In the same way, Israel was to be set apart from the nations and dedicated to God. If the Israelites obeyed God's ways, treating people fairly and honoring Him, they would be blessed. If they didn't, things would not go well for them.

The covenant between God and Abraham became the covenant between God and Israel. The agreement had demanded Abraham's strict adherence to God's word. God did not change His plan and use Ishmael. He insisted Abraham and Sarah obey Him and follow through with His vision for Isaac. Likewise Israel was to honor God and His word only. Through Israel God would teach the world about Himself.

God's agreement with Abraham included the law of blessing and curses, not only for the nation of Israel, but also for others. "And I will bless them that bless thee, and curse him that curseth thee: and in thee shall all families of the earth be blessed." (Genesis 12:3) This extended to Israel as the descendants of Abraham. Nations that blessed Israel would be blessed; nations that treated them badly would be cursed. The curses included sickness, poverty, war and every horrible thing you can think of. Deuteronomy 28 lists the blessings and the curses.

So back to our question, why did God want to take the land away from the Canaanites? We see from God's agreement with Abraham that God requires a standard of behavior. The Canaanites were aware of this standard in ancient days because they were all descended from Noah, the preacher of righteousness. But as years went by, they did not keep this standard. When God made the agreement with Abraham, He said the time was not yet full for the Canaanites. God was giving them more time to change their ways.

While Abraham was walking around Canaan, Noah's son Shem was still alive. Remember, Abraham was his direct descendant. Through Shem's testimony there was still a witness to God's standard of behavior.

Then 430 years passed. The Canaanites hadn't improved their behavior. Meanwhile the Israelites had grown into a large population, but they were slaves in Egypt. Finally Moses led the Israelites out of Egypt because the time had come for them to take over Canaan. God wanted to remove the Canaanites from the land because they were wicked. Deut. 9:4 says "… but for the wickedness of these nations the LORD doth drive them out…"

Archaeology has supported the Bible's claim of the Canaanites' wicked society. They practiced tortuous child sacrifice, sexual perversions and idol worship. The Canaanites were a people who had rejected God and His message in the days following Noah's landing of the ark. They created their own religions, beginning in Babylon, and grew worse as time went on. God had given them hundreds of years to change their ways, but they didn't want to. Instead, they magnified their rebellion.

Surely there were other societies just as wicked, you may argue. But this is the place, Jerusalem, where God has chosen to return to and establish His kingdom. This is the chosen land for the chosen nation to introduce Him to the world. That chosen nation is Israel.

Now that we know why God was giving the land to Abraham, let's take a look at the creation of Israel as God ordained it.

We learned that the nation of Israel began with a miraculous birth. Abraham was 100 years old when Isaac was born, and Sarah was 90. Isaac's descendants multiplied into a massive population. They were known by the name Israel, through Abraham's grandson, Jacob. This massive population was organized by twelve tribes. Each one was named for one of Jacob's sons of whom they descended.

Hundreds of years later, when the Israelites were forced to become slaves in Egypt, God delivered them from Pharaoh, their chief slave master, with a series of miracles that resulted in destroying Egypt perhaps during Neferhotep's reign in the 13th dynasty.

According to new research by David Down and others, Egypt did not recover until Thutmose's dynasty in the New Kingdom hundreds of years afterward. Then God continued to provide, protect and defend Israel with…you guessed it, miracles!

You could say that Israel was a nation of miracles. God was still abiding by the agreement He had made with Abraham hundreds of years before. It was with this mass population of slaves that God began to unfold His plan for Israel becoming a nation. At first Israel was a theocracy in which God was the Supreme Ruler and priests led the Israelites.

Israel was a country like no other because the God of the universe began to reveal Himself to them and through them to other nations. The nations of Egypt, Midian, Canaan and beyond began to hear of

Israel's God. Moses' father-in-law declared, "Now I know that the Lord is greater than all gods…" (Exodus 18:11) All the Canaanite kings lost their courage at the news of the Lord's miracles. (Joshua 5:1) Israel's role was to show God's character to the other countries.

God reinstated the covenant agreement with these descendants of Abraham in the Wilderness (Deuteronomy and Leviticus 26) and explained its requirements and consequences. It included multiple blessings in health, wealth and protection categories. As we learned earlier there was only one rule: obey God— period. If they were obedient, the agreement stood. If they weren't, it didn't.

Leviticus 18 is one chapter that warns them if they became wicked, they would get kicked out of the land just like the Canaanites had. The fledgling nation had a rocky start and was demoted to wandering in a desert for forty years. The next generation obeyed a bit better.

After the era of Moses and Joshua, Israel entered a difficult time. This part of Israel's history is recorded in Judges. It quickly became obvious how important a godly leader was to keep them motivated to obey God. When they had one, things were good. When they didn't, things went badly for them…real bad.

Judges has a recurring theme. It states repeatedly, "They did evil in the sight of the Lord," and then describes the mayhem Israel was experiencing. A cycle emerged during this part of their history. The people cried for help; then God appointed one of their own to deliver them from the oppressive power of their neighbors.

The writer finally gives a reason for the madness in Judges 17:6 "…every man did that which was right in his own eyes." This was Israel's season of relative truth which is the idea that there is no absolute truth and everyone can decide for themselves what is right. It created chaos as they separated themselves from God, His blessing, and His truth.

They were still revealing God to the nations, but in the form of what not to do. God had not given up on them. They had given up on Him. Israel wanted to be like everyone else. They were tired of being different, so they asked for a king. And the cycle continued through the history of their monarchy. When the king obeyed God, everything went well for them. When he didn't... Well, you get the idea.

The nation eventually split into two parts, each with its own king. The first to fall was the Northern Kingdom. All their kings disobeyed God, and the Assyrian Empire conquered them. The Southern Kingdom had good kings and bad kings. The bad influences eventually won, and the Southern Kingdom was taken over by the Babylonian Empire. The nation of Israel ended in 586 BC. There were some Israelites left, but they were rulers of the land no more.

This story of the beginning and the end of Israel fills the Old Testament. It includes the history of ancient Israel and its neighbors, their wars, treaties, accomplishments and we can read the words of their kings, poets, prophets and priests.

Romans 15:4 says, "For whatsoever things were written aforetime were written for our learning, that we through patience and comfort of the scriptures might have hope."

And God gave them hope even in exile. He told their prophets that one day He would bring them back to their land. In that future day, they would come from the four corners of the earth, and He would never drive them out again. The Israelites read the words of their prophets and looked forward to that day. Their hope was not in vain because another miracle happened in 1948; a dead nation came back to life. 2,000 years later!

Ezekiel had prophesied that Israel would again be a nation. Ezekiel 37:1-14 describes skeletons growing healthy flesh on them and coming back to life. "Then he said unto me, Son of man, these bones are the whole house of Israel: behold, they say, Our bones are dried, and our hope is lost: we are cut off for our parts. Therefore prophesy and say unto them, Thus saith the Lord GOD; Behold, O my people, I will open your graves, and cause you to come up out of your graves, and bring you into the land of Israel." (Ezekiel 37:11-12)

These skeletons represented the Israelites scattered throughout the earth with no country of their own and that country coming back to life. It was probably not a coincidence that pictures of the suffering and dead Jews in the Holocaust were still fresh in their minds when this prophecy was fulfilled. God knows the future, and when He gave Ezekiel the vision, He knew nothing would seem as hopeless as the Jewish condition after WWII.

But in one day, all was changed. Their "dead" language was also resurrected. The story of Israel becoming a nation is too much to include here, but it is perhaps the biggest sign in our generation that God is still honoring His agreement with them and His word is true.

Israel had a very different culture than its neighbors. This has been one of its major characteristics since its birth. What a people believe about themselves and the world can be seen in the culture they create. A nation's laws tell us a lot about its values and views. Exodus 20-24 and Leviticus are places you can read their laws. A careful reading of them discloses the differences between Israel and its neighbors.

The rich and poor in Israel had equal status under the law– even the foreigners among them. Women and slaves were granted rights. Provisions were made for the poor and needy.

Punishments were equal to the crime, not a person's status in society. Other cultures' laws gave special treatment to the wealthy. The rich got off easy if guilty, but punishments for the poor could be brutal for minor crimes—especially if committed against the rich.

Moses is accused by some scholars and historians of copying another set of laws called Hammurabi's Code. But it is important to know that modern archaeological discoveries are leading some archaeologists to place Hammurabi after Moses, eliminating the argument that Moses copied Hammurabi's Code.

But Hammurabi's code was unfair. It treated the rich with favor if they were guilty of crimes. The poor were dealt harsh penalties for even small crimes as in other cultures. So even if the argument is that Moses copied the laws, then it also must be admitted he greatly improved them. But Moses didn't invent these laws. God gave them to him, and we can see God's love, mercy and protection in them.

Contrary to other nation's laws, everyone in Israel had value. For example, if you stole something, you repaid its value regardless of the status of the victim. No one killed you or chopped off your hand. An eye for an eye refers to a standard of law whether you were rich or poor, citizen or foreigner. This was a standard for justice, not a declaration of revenge.

Also, a woman accused of adultery was not left to men to decide her fate. God would reveal the truth of her guilt or innocence and men had to abide by His verdict, not their wishes or feelings. Women could own property too and were not to be used. It was a society others wanted to join. When the Israelite slaves left Egypt, some of the Egyptians went with them. Rahab wanted in. Ruth wanted in. There must have been others who wanted in because Acts 2:10 mentions converts. Israel was an oasis for mercy and justice in the ancient world.

The most important thing to know about Israel, is that it was from this people group and this society Jesus was born. God's original call to Abraham included, "and in thee shall all families of the earth be blessed." Jesus' arrival on the earth fulfilled this covenant promise. Again, a miraculous birth, miraculous deliverance, miraculous acts and a resurrection marked Jesus' life as God walking the earth. Jesus expanded the agreement with Abraham to include the "Whosoevers."

When Jesus said, "It is finished" while He was on the cross, He referred to the work started in Genesis 3 of a promised Savior. That work continued through the expanded agreement with Abraham and Sarah of a righteousness by faith for anyone who believes God to make them right with Him. Like Abraham, one has to believe that what God says He will do. The people who believe, from any nationality or class, are the Whosoevers.

The old agreement of blessings still applied, but a few new ones were added. Like the Holy Spirit. Jesus said, "Verily, verily, I say unto you, he that heareth my word, and believeth on Him that sent me, hath everlasting life, and shall not come into condemnation; but is passed from death unto life." (John 5:24)

God's expanded new agreement stood as an invitation, now not just to Israel, but to the whole world. Through Abraham's descendants, through Israel and only Israel, God had brought the greatest gift to men everywhere, and the invitation continues until the earth ends. This is the story of the New Testament.

Christianity would not only bring the message of Jesus and salvation to the world, it would open knowledge and creativity to the academic and art world, growth to society and scientific development.

But Christianity began with Jewish men preaching Jesus. There have always been Jews who have believed in Jesus as their Savior. In the 1960s and 1970s, however, the numbers of Messianic Jews, as they are called, increased. In 1967, after the Jews took back Jerusalem from the Jordanians in the Six-Day War, interest in Jesus sparked. According to

Jews for Jesus in the 21st century, there are 250,000 Messianic Jews in the US, 20,000 in Israel, and 350,000 world-wide.

There are 6 million Jews living in Israel. The total world population for Jews was 16.5 million in 2015. The population has finally rebounded from the Holocaust because that was how many there were before WWII.

Soon after Christianity took hold in the first century, an attitude began to creep into some Gentile (non-Jewish) believers. It became an idea called Replacement Theology, and it gained steam around the time of Emperor Constantine. This theology stated Christian believers, or the Church as they are called, took the place of Israel as the chosen people of God. It may have seemed like it. The Israelites were scattered all over, their Temple was destroyed by Rome, and they had no country. Many Jews didn't even acknowledge Jesus.

In Romans 11, Paul had already addressed this mindset, however. He reminded the Gentile Christians that they were grafted in, added to an existing group, and even though they were blessed because Israel rejected its Savior, God fully intended to make them right with Him. In fact, Paul says that Jews are the root out of which Christians grow.

God will never break His agreement with Abraham. Jesus foretold all what would happen when He said, "And they [Israel] shall fall by the edge of the sword, and shall be led away captive into all nations: and Jerusalem shall be trodden down of the Gentiles, until the times of the Gentiles be fulfilled." (Luke 21:24) 1948 was one sign that the times of the Gentiles were over.

The flow of Jews back to the land of Israel began in the late 1800s. The land lay desolate. Mark Twain (The Innocents Abroad) and others who visited the Holy Land described it as barren and sparsely populated. The rise of Islam had changed the culture of the Middle East.

In the late 7th century, the Dome of the Rock was constructed over the site of Solomon's Temple. Jewish scholars believe it to be built on the stone Abraham prepared to offer Isaac and the Holy of Holies section of the First and Second Temples.

According to *Bible Study Tools*, the inscription on the Dome's ceiling states Jesus was not crucified (it only appeared that way), God has no Son and there is no Trinity, there is no need for the people of earth to be redeemed, salvation is by works and Muhammad is greater than Jesus.

Scholars debate the reason for the Dome's construction. It is not a mosque but a shrine. Another mosque was erected nearby to honor Muhammad's supposed ascension to heaven. But Jews and Christians generally do not miss the intent to contradict their beliefs and elevate the Islamic religion. Joseph Farah points out that there are no holy sites in Israel that have anything to do with Islam. Jerusalem is not even mentioned in the Qur'an.

But Arabic Muslims are not about to concede their claim to the Temple Mount. They are gaining support from nations like China, France, Germany, New Zealand, Sweden and others.

Modern Israel is a diverse melting pot of Jews who have come back to their homeland from places like Russia, Morocco, Yemen, Egypt, Europe and America. The current Prime Minister, Benjamin Netanyahu, is the first prime minister since 1948 to have been born in Israel. It is his job to juggle the constant barrage of attacks from the hostile populations inside and outside his country.

God made it clear that anyone who curses Israel will themselves be cursed. (Genesis 12:1-3) But jealousy and hatred towards Israel has always existed. Israel is strategically located in the center of the Middle East, surrounded by neighbors whose wish is for it to be obliterated. On March 9, 2016, *Newsweek* ran an article by Jack Moore titled, "Iran

Tests Ballistic Missiles Carrying The Message 'Israel Must Be Wiped Out.' "

In the beginning of this chapter we asked why God had chosen Abraham. It wasn't because Abraham was smarter, taller, more fit or rich. Abraham was chosen because he believed God and he trusted Him to do what He said He would do. The rest of his blessings came after—and because— he believed and trusted God. The result of his belief was the creation of the Hebrew society and religion, and those who share Abraham's faith are heirs of the agreement. (Galatians 3)

Israel gave the world the answers to man's most probing questions, "Who am I and why am I here?" No other philosophy comes close. Israel gave the world its first equal, just and compassionate society; its technological inventions have benefited the world, and most importantly, it introduced us to God through Hebrew men and women telling their stories compiled into a book we call the Bible.

God chose the nation of Israel to make Himself known to us. He placed His son into a tribe and family, so that all people of every nation, tribe and tongue could make Him their Lord and Savior.

Israel continues to amaze and bless the world. In the seventy years it has existed in the modern era, it has risen from ruins and wasteland, amid dire threats, to be one of the most successful countries in the Middle East.

In October 2017, Israeli intelligence forces discovered a Russian act of espionage against the United States. It immediately contacted the U.S. That's a blessing.

Modern Israel is a mix of beliefs branching off from the original Hebrew religion. Some people, though identifying as a Jew for tradition or patriotism, are secular. These are those surrounded by holy sites, ruins from the biblical age, archaeological finds, testifying Christians and modern day miracles. In a sense, they are numb to God's presence and blind to His work.

Jesus stood looking over Jerusalem and spoke these words, "O Jerusalem, Jerusalem, thou that killest the prophets, and stonest them which are sent unto thee, how often would I have gathered thy children together, even as a hen gathereth her chickens under her wings, and ye would not! " (Matthew 23:37)

But they will gather to Him. The book of Revelation promises it. And, since all the rest He said about Israel happened, we can be sure that day is coming, for them and us. We can trust the words of His prophets, Ezekiel, Daniel, Zechariah, John and others.

In the last chapter of this book, we will discuss more about Israel's rightful and eternal borders. But for now, let us acknowledge Israel's place of honor among Jesus' followers around the world.

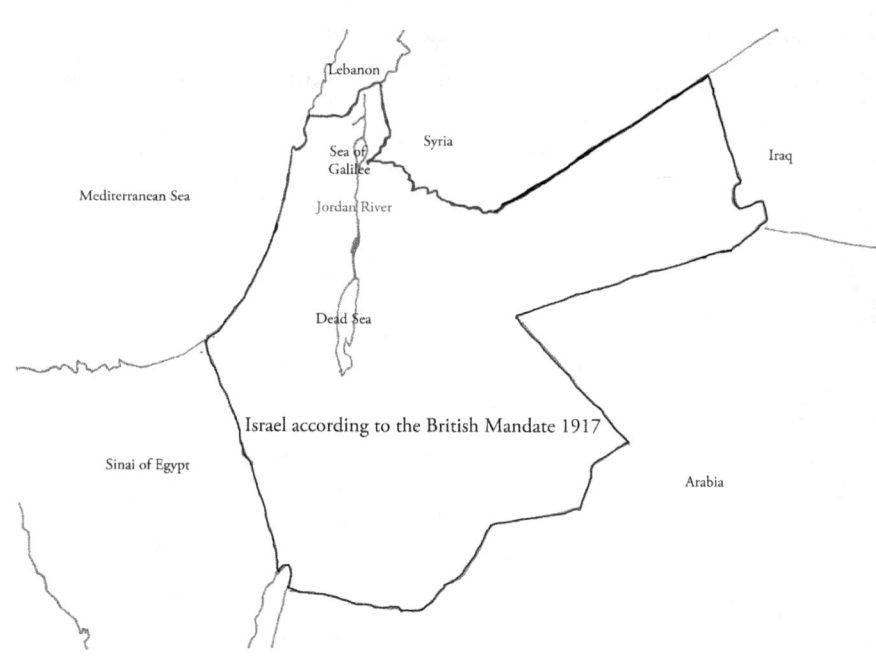

• Chapter 3 •

Palestine

Israel is incorrectly called Palestine. Newscasters, world leaders, educators and a host of others refer to Israel this way. Ignoring the truth, continuing to use the term, only fuels a raging debate.

World governments have been trying to solve a problem in the Middle East they call the Israeli-Palestinian Conflict. It involves two groups of people, the Israelis and the Palestinians, and began around the time that Israel became a nation in 1948.

It seems to be a complicated dilemma where compromises have been made to no avail. The only solution the world sees is to create two nations or states out of Israel, one for Israelis and one for Palestinians. But many experts do not agree. A host of Israelis don't either. They claim, rightly, that land has been surrendered but no peace gained.

The true story is not the main story told on the evening news. Journalists like Joseph Farah, however, insist on telling it. It is a conflict that reaches all the way back to Abraham and the promise God gave him. Let's take a look at the real story behind the trouble.

A recent news item is a fence in the city of Hebron, Israel between the Jewish and Palestinian sections. Abraham built an altar near Hebron. Today Hebron is a city with 220,000 Arabs and 1,000 Jews. It is located in the Judean Mountains in the southern part of the West Bank.

To read the Palestinian side of the story (*PalestinianPortal.org*), one would understand the Israelis to be cruel racists whose goal is to separate the Palestinians and oppress them in an area known for its poor schools, bad economy and crumbling roads.

The Jerusalem Post tells a different story. Tovah Lazaroff writes in his article, that the city split by agreement in 1997 with the Palestinians controlling 80%. The current mayor is a Palestinian who killed six Israelis in a terror attack. Lazaroff states that the Israelis living in the area are the ones that were oppressed, and the Israeli settlers will now be able to govern themselves. He never mentions the fence.

Whose side is closer to the truth? A little digging into the fence story unearths the facts. The mayor is a Palestinian, Sheikh Tayseer Abu Sneineh, and a convicted terrorist. The fence is not new. Construction began in 2000 in response to Palestinian terrorist attacks. The Palestinians increased their assault against Israel in what was called the Second Infitada. The fence was expanded in 2015-16. Attacks have declined. The United Nations states the wall violates international law. Other Middle Eastern nations have similar walls, however.

The West Bank has an interesting history of its own. Emir Abdullah of Mecca, Saudi Arabia was a descendant of Muhammad's great-grandfather. In 1922 during negotiations with Britain, he argued for his right to the region that would become Jordan. He wanted an independent Arab empire. Hoping to make his dream of an Arab kingdom a reality, he planned to take over Syria and Iraq, where his brothers had lost control, and Lebanon, adding them to his family's holdings in Arabia.

Britain coaxed him to wait. They were friends as Abdullah had helped them overthrow the Ottomans. In 1923, Britain established his rule over the Emirate of Transjordan which made the proposed country of Israel much smaller. Unlike his Muslim friends, Abdullah wasn't against Israel because he preferred to be neighbors with them over the Palestinians. (It was a stance that caused his assassination in 1951 by a Palestinian.)

Egypt and other Arab countries did not trust Abdullah. He needed to improve his reputation, so the day after Israel became a nation, Abdullah joined Egypt, Syria, Lebanon and Iraq to fight Israel. He took the West Bank and part of Jerusalem in an act that was considered illegal by world governments at the time. (Arab-Israeli War 1948.) It also annoyed Egypt.

Following the war, he granted Jordanian citizenship to Arabs living in the West Bank in an effort to gain their loyalty. But the Israelis won it back from the Jordanians in 1967 in the Six-Day War. Mounting Palestinian turmoil made Jordan sever all ties with the West Bank's Arabs years later.

The land in the West Bank includes part of Judea of the former Israelite Southern Kingdom and Samaria of the former Northern Kingdom. It is territory allotted to Israel by agreements prior to 1948. The important thing to learn is that the Palestinians had no standing army or government of their own in the 1920s, 1940s, 1950s or 1960s in a territory they claim they owned. And, they were offered citizenship in a Muslim nation.

You may be wondering why Palestinians want to attack Israel. Isn't the country of Israel called Palestine? Let's start with who the Palestinians are and why they think they are the rightful owners of the land.

Who are the Palestinians?

Yasser Arafat was an important Palestinian leader. He claimed to be a descendant of ancient Canaanites. He said his family were Jebusites, the ancient people of Jerusalem. A *National Geographic* article by Stefan Lovgren disputes his claim. "… if you tried to do a DNA test on Arafat, you would be hard pressed to prove that he has any Jebusite blood running through his veins."

The article goes on to say what many other experts have said: the people who call themselves Palestinians migrated to the area from Saudi Arabia and Yemen during the Muslim conquests of the 5th century. Arafat himself was born in Egypt and moved to Jerusalem.

A recent article on DNA testing does link the Canaanites with people in Lebanon, however. There are Palestinians in Lebanon, but they moved in during the 1960s. Could they have married people descending from the Canaanites?

Possibly. Intermarriage between tribes even in ancient times was common. It always has been. But that doesn't strengthen their argument according to the Bible or even history. Canaanites were distant cousins of the Israelites and were not included in the promise God made to Abraham about the land of Israel. (Genesis 12:1-3; Genesis 15:7)

The word Palestine is not in the Bible. Its meaning is, however. Palestine is related to the Hebrew word, *Plishtiy*. It is their word for Philistine, and it means immigrant. It is first used in Genesis 10:14 and identifies them with ancient Egyptians. Archaeology has linked the Philistines with Greek culture which is understandable concerning their location or may be part of a larger history we don't know yet.

These people settled near the coast but migrated inland and were enemies of Israel for a long time. They are not listed with those who were Canaanites and are not mentioned in historical records after the Assyrian and Babylonian Empires conquered their cities.

So, are the Palestinians Philistines? No.

Around 132 AD, the Jews revolted against the Romans and took over important strongholds. This event is called the Bar Kokhba Revolt. Emperor Hadrian had harassed and persecuted them but never expected them to retaliate successfully. Finally he put down the revolt, but still angry, he scattered them everywhere.

He banned most of their religious practices and renamed Jerusalem *Aelia Capitolina*. As a final insult, he renamed Judea after one of Israel's most hated enemies. He called it *Palestinia* which is Latin for Philistine. Israel was then referred to as Palestine. It was meant to humiliate the Israelis. And if there were a "Palestinian people" they were the small population of Jews that remained in the area.

But the name stuck. In 1917 in the Balfour Declaration, Britain announced their intent to "establish a national home for the Jews in Palestine." They hoped that bringing in Jews would improve the economy and quiet Arab hostility toward Jews.

After WWI when the land was being considered for Israel by the Peel Commission, the first choice had been a united country of Palestinians. But party members did not acknowledge a people called Palestinians. In fact, Arabs and Israelis declared there were no Palestinian people.

The Peel Commission was trying to appease Arabs who didn't want Jews to have a country. Those arguing for a Palestinian state were Arabs. Awni Abd al-Hadi was a founding member of the al-Fatat (Young Arab Society). He worked towards Arab independence and testified that the Jews had invented the idea of Palestine and that it had always been part of Syria.

The British solution was to divide the land between them, the much smaller portion going to Israel. The larger section would go to their trusted friend, Emir Abdullah. As you can guess, that wasn't popular. But the reason may surprise you. The Arab groups wanted it *all*.

The Jews did make Palestine prosperous. Tensions were rising against the Jews, however. The 1920s and 1930s proved difficult for them. By 1936 they were being persecuted in Germany and Poland. The same year they were attacked in their homeland by rioting anti-Jew Arabs. Over three hundred Jews were wounded and eighty were killed.

The Peel Commission stated the reasons for the unrest in Palestine during these decades were hatred for the Jews. Because of this, no land agreements were ever satisfactory because Arabs did not want Jews to have land. Period. An important fact gleaned from the British documents is that no homeland for a non-Jewish people called Palestinians was mentioned during this era. The only non-Jewish people recognized by all parties involved were Arabs.

That never stopped people from calling themselves Palestinians, however. The Palestinian Liberation Organization (PLO) formed in 1964 in response to the Arab League and others who were hoping to unify their leadership. After their defeat in the Six-Day War, the Arabs needed a strong leader more than ever. After splitting into factions, the PLO chose Yasser Arafat as the chairman to ride out the next decades' efforts to establish a legitimate reputation for the Arab effort to reclaim Israel.

But in a meeting with Palestinian leaders in 1976, Syrian President Hafez al-Assad reminded Arafat that there was no Palestine because it was part of Syria. "There is no such thing as a Palestinian people, there is no Palestinian entity; there is only Syria." Later he kicked Arafat out of Syria and banned him from returning. Of course, both Arab leaders wanted the land of Israel for themselves. Earlier, 1970-71, Abdullah's grandson King Hussein of Jordan had ousted the Palestinians from his country because they were trying to take Jordan from him. Apparently, they didn't want to be citizens; they wanted to be rulers. Undaunted, they went to Lebanon and caused a civil war there.

So what can we conclude from the research? Palestinians are Arabs and even the Arabs declared it so.

Why Do Arabs Want Israel's Land?

The land was sparsely populated and barren after Muslims controlled the region called Palestine. Visitors to the area in the late 1800s affirm this fact and so do British records after WWI. A French photographer named, Felix Bonfils, traveled through the area. His pictures show a deserted mosque with grass growing through the paved area, a lot of Jews, but no permanent Palestinian settlements. Mark Twain, among other celebrities of the day, visited what they called the Holy Land. Twain wrote about his journeys in *The Innocents Abroad*:

> Of all the lands there are for dismal scenery, I think Palestine must be the prince. The hills are barren, they are dull of color, they are unpicturesque in shape. The valleys are unsightly deserts fringed with a feeble vegetation that has an expression about it of being sorrowful and despondent… Palestine sits in sackcloth and ashes. … about whose borders nothing grows but weeds, and scattering tufts of cane, and that treacherous fruit that promises refreshment to parching lips, but turns to ashes at the touch. Nazareth is forlorn;

about that ford of Jordan where the hosts of Israel entered the Promised Land with songs of rejoicing, one finds only a squalid camp of fantastic Bedouins of the desert... (Chapter LVI page 452.)

It doesn't sound like a thriving metropolis of Arabs some want us to believe. In fact the Arabs there were described as deadly. A *New York Times* article published March 10, 1858, written by a pastor working at an agricultural mission described an event of murder and rape that shocked the civilized world. But attacks by Arab raiders were not uncommon.

In the chapter on Israel, we learned that Jews began returning to Israel in the late 1800s. They returned to places like the Mother of Jewish Settlements where a group of Jews living in Jerusalem settled on the plains of Sharon (share- own). These Jews arriving from Europe began enlarging the communities of Jews who had never left. Even a group of sturdy Americans from Maine built a settlement in Jaffa because they wanted to help the Jewish people.

Egyptians were also moving to the area. During the late 1700s, a famine in Egypt drove people north. In fact, more than once Egyptians fled to "Palestine" to avoid war, forced labor and natural disasters. Some Egyptians were brought there to be slaves under Ottoman rule. None of these migrants established a thriving empire in the region proper.

By the descriptions of the land in British records and by other visitors, we can believe the reports that the people faced many obstacles. Moshe Aumann, in his book *Land Ownership in Palestine 1880-1948*, describes the conditions in detail. He writes that Arabic Bedouins chased struggling Arab peasants out of the land and the Turkish Ottoman Empire did nothing to stop it.

The Arab peasants sold their land to wealthier Arabs who pocketed the money with no intentions of farming or herding. It is true then, that "Palestinian" peasants were displaced, but not by Jews. Their fellow Arabs displaced them.

The state of Arabs who remained was deplorable. Aumann quotes the *Report of the Palestine Royal Commission of the Maritime Plain in 1913*:

> The road leading from Gaza to the north was only a summer track suitable for transport by camels and carts . . . no orange groves, orchards or vineyards were to be seen until one reached Yabna village. . . . Not in a single village in all this area was water used for irrigation. . . . Houses were all of mud. No windows were anywhere to be seen. . . . The ploughs used were of wood. . . . The yields were very poor. . . . The sanitary conditions in the village were horrible. Schools did not exist. . . . The rate of infant mortality was very high... The western part, towards the sea, was almost a desert. . . . The villages in this area were few and thinly populated. Many ruins of villages were scattered over the area, as owing to the prevalence of malaria, many villages were deserted by their inhabitants. (Appendix 2, pg. 118.)

The malaria ridden sections were the first the Jews bought. They redirected water, fought off Bedouins and began farming successfully. They purchased their land from Arabs living in Syria who had deserted what their ancestors had taken in Muslim conquests. Arabs saw a great opportunity and sold desert wasteland to Jews for 1,000 dollars an acre.

The Jews continued to flourish and Isaiah's prophecy (35:2) about the desert blooming became a reality. Aumann points out that this was the beginning of the end for the Muslim feudal system, and it annoyed the Arabs. They were losing control.

The Jewish population increased. A census taken by the Turkish government in 1875 stated that the majority of the population in Jerusalem was Jews. As the population grew and agricultural success turned into financial success and established societies, Arab Muslims stopped smirking about their wasteland-for-gold scandal and realized the Jews' plans for permanent settlements were possible.

This was alarming to Arabs for multiple reasons. But the main one, upon which every argument over the land spins, is Arab Muslims do not want Israel to exist in any form. This sentiment was expressed before the Six-Day War in 1967 by Egyptian President Gamal Abdel Nasser. "We will not accept any...coexistence with Israel...Today the issue is not the establishment of peace between the Arab states and Israel....The war with Israel is in effect since 1948."

Iraqi President Araf added, "The existence of Israel is an error which must be rectified. This is our opportunity to wipe out the ignominy which has been with us since 1948. Our goal is clear -- to wipe Israel off the map." Jordan, Syria, Lebanon, Kuwait, Sudan, Saudi Arabia and Algeria joined in with Russian support.

Nothing has changed in the Arabic mind for fifty years. To sum up their feelings, a modern Palestinian hit song (pun intended) is titled, "I'm Coming Towards You My Enemy," and in a catchy Arabic tune declares, "I'm coming towards you, my enemy with rifles, cleavers and knives." Other popular tunes are "Jerusalem is Bleeding," and "Stab the Zionist and Say God is Great." No warning labels for violence on the CDs are required. On the contrary. This is the promoted music for young Arabs.

Palestinian authorities reward these kinds of attacks against Jews and Christians with large sums of money, health care, housing and other benefits. If the offender is killed, their family's award increases. Streets have been named for terrorists.

The answer to the question, "Why Do Arabs Want Israel's Land?" is they don't. The key to understanding Arab conflicts with Israel is to realize all the fighting is not about the land. It is about Israel as a people.

Another puzzling thing happened in the years following the fall of the Ottoman Empire and the rise of successful Jewish development following WWI. Arabs began moving back into the land of Israel because the standard of living was better there than in their home countries.

Again the British recorded the facts in their reports. Aumann writes that they included a special section to address the illegal Arab immigration. (Appendix 2pg. 124) Illegal Arab migration?

Arafat traveled the world, identifying Palestinians as an indigenous culture living for thousands of years in the land of Israel before the Israelis. He claimed the Israelis took over the Palestinians vast, flourishing settlements and society. Israelis were and are named Illegal Occupants, and much of the world still believes that story as the history of the area.

But actual history tells another story. Archeology tells another story as it uncovers artifacts from Israel's ancient kings before the Muslim culture existed. The story is Palestinians never were sovereigns or controlled the land of Israel. UNESCO is the cultural heritage protection arm of the United Nations. They deny any connection to Israel and Jerusalem or the Temple Mount. To do that, they have to ignore what the ground is telling the world through the thousands of ancient artifacts and inscriptions establishing Israeli history. The United Nations is pushing to stop archaeological activities in Israel. Why?

Recent conflicts in the area center in Hebron, Gaza, and the West Bank. In 2005 Israel pulled out of the Gaza Strip and the Palestinian terrorist group, Hamas, moved in. Lebanon accuses the Palestinians of starting their civil war in the 1960s and 70s from which they've never recovered. Lebanon is controlled by Hamas and Hezbollah, the Iranian terrorist group. According to Lebanon, Palestinians have a history of being disruptive.

Palestinian refugees are refugees because Jordan is the only Arab country in the Middle East who offers them citizenship. Recently, they've been revoking that privilege because they are afraid of being outnumbered. Israel will grant them citizenship, but it suppresses their patriotism for reasons of self-defense.

Many Palestinians refuse Israel's offer, however, because an Israeli citizenship does not bode well for that person in an Arab culture that dislikes Jews. Abdullah was killed for his relationship with Israel. He was shot on the steps of the Al-Aqsa mosque, and was one of three moderate Muslim leaders to die for their views during that era.

Most Palestinians want a Palestinian state, but few would want to live there. Living conditions in Palestinian controlled areas is poor. Our "Fence in Hebron" story attests to that–except the conditions are blamed on the Israelis.

So, if we've answered who the Palestinians are (Arabs that other Arabs don't like) and we've found out their objections are not really concerned with land but the Jewish people, maybe we should ask a new question.

Why do Palestinians hate Israelis?

Anti-Semitism is defined as hostility or prejudice against Jews. But the anti-Semitism in the Middle East is more than prejudice. It is spiritual. The conflict must be understood with each party's religion in mind because the conflict is becoming more religiously motivated.

We learned that Arabs also claim their ancestry from Abraham, from his sons Ishmael, Zimran, Jokshan, Medan, Midian, Ishbak, Shuah and their descendants. Many of these people became Muslims when Muhammad founded Islam.

The tenets of Islam have very little tolerance for non-Muslims. While Christians are infidels, Jews are monkeys, pigs and infidels. They need to be exterminated to purify the land.

There are some Jews who are tired of tolerating those they consider trouble-makers, idol worshippers and invaders and have committed violence against Palestinians. They too would rid Israel of them to purify the land.

This purifying the land idea is mentioned in the Old Testament. One example is 2Chronicles 34:8. The differences in the definition of what and who is pure concerning Judaism and Islam creates the conflict.

There are more Jews who are tolerant and would agree to an independent Palestinian State, but tolerant Muslims are not tolerated by their religious leaders. Therefore, there will never be a Palestinian State existing alongside Israel.

Increased violence shows that the religious side of the conflict is getting stronger for both parties. The policy in which Palestinians are honored and paid to kill Jews is called Pay to Slay. This policy has shocked some of the countries favorable to the Palestinians.

David Wood ("Three Qur'an Verses Every Jew Should Know") gives a brief but accurate history of the relations between Jews and Muslims. When Muhammad began receiving his visions and writing them down as the Qur'an, he affirmed the Torah and the Bible, declaring that these three religions, Judaism, Christianity and Islam are together the religions against all idol worshippers.

When Muhammad recited his sermons to the Jews in Medina, they rejected his revelations. Then the Qur'an was modified. Christianity and Islam stood together against Jews and idol worshippers. Alas, Christians also rejected Muhammad's new religion.

After that, Muhammad revised the Qur'an again. The revised edition is the essence of the version which continues today that says everyone is an infidel unless they accept Islam. Even then there may be exceptions. Muslims don't like other Muslims either. But Jews must be killed until they are all dead which will usher in the Islamic rendering of the end times. This could be seen in the violence during 2017 as the fighting in Jerusalem intensified.

Sadly, Christian Palestinians as well as other Middle Eastern Christians can hate Jews as well. Ted Cruz was booed during a speech about solidarity with Israel by Middle Eastern Christians in 2014. A Pew Research study on *Global Attitudes in 2011* found only 4% of Palestinians had a favorable view of Jews. Also, they were split identifying themselves with their nationality 43% or their religion 40%.

If the Pew study is correct, hating Jews is the practice of Qur'an believing Muslim Palestinians and patriotic Palestinians. If that conclusion is correct, how might it affect peace talks between Palestine and Israel?

The problem is far from over and will never be solved. Yes, that is right. It will never be solved by men. The book of Revelation reveals how all disputes will be settled in *one day*. (More on that in the last chapter.) Remember God's promise to everyone that if you bless Israel, you will be blessed? If only the Palestinians could accept that promise and act on it. Their life would be very different.

Let's Review

Palestine is a word the Romans used to aggravate the Jews. Poor people of mixed heritage, Arab certainly, were caught between their own Arabic countrymen taking advantage of them. But they found a solution in the rise of the Jewish society again coming to a place of influence in the land. Soon, they wanted the land for themselves and identified themselves as Palestinians. Arab against Arab against Israeli conflicts drive the unrest in the Middle East.

Genesis 21:22-31 tells about an agreement a Philistine king made with Abraham. It included water rights to a well Abraham dug in Beersheba. The agreement and water rights were to pass down to successive generations in Abraham's family.

In Genesis 26, the story turns to Isaac. A famine inspired Isaac to move south for a while, but by God's direction he stopped in Philistine territory where he met the king's family that his father had known and had made the agreement concerning water rights. While there, Isaac became so wealthy, in a time of famine, that the Philistines were jealous. They filled the wells Abraham had dug with dirt.

Then the king asked Isaac to leave because he was too powerful. He left and continued to dig wells that the Philistines continued to fill. Apparently the agreement to water rights was not going to be honored.

Finally, Isaac settled far enough away that the Philistines quit harassing him.

Then the Philistine king came to visit him. Isaac wondered why since it was the king who had sent him away. Apparently the king was afraid Isaac would attack him or in some way harm his people. He wanted to make a treaty with Isaac to benefit himself.

It is a similar story of the early returning Jews to the land called "Palestine." But this was their land, Israel, given to them by God. In the early days of their return it was not the Egyptian-Greek Philistines who harassed and took advantage; it was an Arabic people living in a land named for Israel's ancient enemy.

But God's covenant agreement with Abraham prevailed in 1948. Even though the name Palestine is recognized as a name for the region, God will not honor it as such. He calls it Israel and will someday expand its borders to the area He designated as the rightful borders of His chosen nation.

• Chapter 4 •

Islamic Terrorism

Terrorism is not new. The Assyrians used it to build an empire. They sent messengers to townspeople and kings, threatening horrific tortures, and had a reputation for backing up those threats. Visible signs of their violent attacks, impaled bodies etc., lined streets, decorated gates of cities and instilled terror into a population. The Assyrians won many victories without drawing a sword because they used fear to obtain surrender.

Assyria was a country with an army, but examples of fear forcing a person to react in a certain way abound in everyday life. Being the victim of bullying and abuse are examples on one end of the scale while the fear of being disciplined by a parent or an authority figure like a policeman is on the other.

The fear of failure or disease may encourage one to act a certain way. We may conclude then that "fear" can be a motivator used for bad and good purposes. Fear may be used to harm, bully and abuse or instill respect to set safe boundaries and guidelines.

This positive aspect is not defined as true fear but honor or respect for certain persons or advice. One can recognize the position of the individual or truth of the advice and is aware of outcomes that could happen. Then they make a decision on what they want to happen instead of what they don't want to happen. Obeying authority figures whether it is a parent's curfew, speed limits or diet and exercise suggestions are in this honor and revere category.

The Bible uses the word fear this way when it says, "And the LORD commanded us to do all these statutes, to fear the LORD our God, for our good always, that he might preserve us alive, as it is at this day." (Deuteronomy 6:24) Or, "And his mercy is on them that fear him from generation to generation." (Luke 1:50) There are many more like this, but you get the idea: respect and honor God.

This type of honoring and respect is due authorities, and especially God, because they are setting those boundaries for our protection and well being. The consequences of violating those boundaries or guidelines are brought about by our choice because we did not honor authority. The Israelites struggled with this concept throughout the Bible.

This type of reverent fear is not what we are talking about when we speak of bullying or abuse. There is nothing good about those behaviors, and there is nothing good about terrorism.

In this chapter, we are going to focus on the negative aspect of fear as a motivator and its use in the act of terrorism because terrorism is a constant threat in the Middle East. But first let's look at how the word terror is used in the news when it is referred to as terrorism.

Terror is extreme fear. Terrorism consists of a manipulator, the terrorist, and a manipulatee, the victim. *Newsweek* published an article by Cristina Maza on February 26, 2018. The article talks about attacks on government buildings and civilians in various African cities. In one attack 800 civilians were killed by groups fighting for their political and religious ideals.

Michael Holden reported on *Reuters* March 2, 2018, that Umar Haque, a teacher living in London, was caught training children in acts of terrorism. He taught them how to attack and kill people in shopping malls, stores, banks and how to target soldiers and police officers. He also taught them how to wage attacks at larger attractions such as the Big Ben Tower.

Haque even discussed how to carry out successful attacks using guns and car bombs with another teacher. His reason? Besides seeking a well rounded education for his students? He supported ISIS, the political and religious group responsible for the deaths of thousands.

In these two articles we see the *Oxford Dictionary's* definition of terrorism: "The unlawful use of violence and intimidation, especially against civilians, in the pursuit of political aims." Two specific tactics label the action as terrorism— violence and intimidation. While intimidation has always been a tactic of war, terrorism is regarded as barbaric among civilized populations.

It is used to force people to submit to a governing body and its ideas. Terrorists target unarmed civilians to instill fear in a society and to force submission or evacuation. These civilians would not support the government or its ideas willingly which is why force is needed to obtain the terrorists' goal.

We will focus on terrorism in the context of the Middle East. With this in mind, the question may be asked, "Why are most terrorists Islamic?" The quick answer is that while Islam is a religion, it can become a political governing body. But it gets complicated. Let's start with the beginning.

The History of Islam

The history of Islam begins with a man named Muhammad. Muhammad was born in Mecca around 570 AD. Mecca is in the country of Saudi Arabia today. An orphan from a wealthy tribe, Muhammad became a successful merchant and married a woman fifteen years older. The area was under the influence of the kingdom of Himyar, a Jewish and Christian empire based in Yemen. Yet, the city of Mecca was a center of worship dedicated to 360 gods and goddesses, including one named Allah and his wife named Al-Lat. This goddess is identified as Allah's daughter in some stories. He also has other daughters, Uzza and Manāt.

Al-Lat is connected to the goddess, Asherah, and represented as a star. (Asherah is a Canaanite god mentioned in the Bible.) According to the *Encyclopedia Britannica*, Al-Lat was worshipped in Mecca at the Ka'bah (cube) in the form of a cube shaped rock. Her worshippers walked in circles around her, chanting praise verses. Dr. Patricia Moneghan states that Al-Lat's name is essentially the same as Allah: the god. The ancient Nabateans made a yearly trip to worship Al-Lat at the Ka'bah. Al-Lat was worshipped in some form as far north as Syria.

When Muhammad was about forty he had a vision of an angel that he said tried to squeeze the air out of him. He was terrified and became suicidal. He thought he had met a *jinn*, a demon. His wife (and her cousin) convinced him it was the angel Gabriel. This angel reappeared in terrifying visions, giving him words that he wrote down. (When he wasn't trying to kill himself.) Muhammad included the worship of Al-Lat in his writings. His family worshipped her at the Ka'bah, where they presided over the religious ceremonies. Later, he proclaimed Allah to be the only god.

At first his revelations were thought of as poetry. But in time his demands to promote Allah provoked the polytheistic Arabs. They did not want to stop worshipping Al-Lat. After enduring persecution due to his insults of other gods, Muhammad left Mecca for the rich, Jewish city of Yathrib which he renamed Medina, an Aramaic word that means law.

At Medina Muhammad became a religious and political leader. He unified the Arabs there by faith in Allah instead of their former allegiances to family and clan. His new religion was called Islam which means submission.

The first version of his religion declared the Book of Moses was accurate, and he referred to it to make just decisions. (Qur'an 46:12) The Book of Moses is the Jewish Torah. He thought his worship of Allah would please Christians and Jews. But neither group understood Allah as the God of the Bible or the Torah. Because he wasn't.

After the people in these towns rejected his new religion, Muhammad conducted raids and began invading Jewish and Christian settlements in Saudi Arabia. They still refused to worship Allah as the one true god. He also began adding to his writings, including the idea of jihad and the submission of non-Muslims. He called his writings the Qur'an.

The Qur'an was continually being added to and adapted to fit the needs of Muhammad's soldiers or himself. For example, it was wrong to have sex with married women (whom they took captive) before they sold them into slavery. It was wrong only until the Qur'an was amended and permitted it.

Muhammad himself could be kind, could be merciful– along with being perverse, greedy for conquest and vengeful against those who criticized him or his ideas. Whether he planned his political purpose for Islam while in Mecca as some ancient texts say or formed his views in Medina is not certain. It is known that he used violence to crush the opposition.

Are Allah and God the same? No. Allah is not the Heavenly Father and he has no son. He is not The Father, the Son [Jesus] and the Holy Spirit. Muslims consider these characteristics of God blasphemous. Allah means god. But Allah cannot be used for the name of the Jewish and Christian God, I AM. They are two different personalities.

Was the angel that appeared to Muhammad the same Gabriel in the Bible? No. The biblical Gabriel may have induced fear by his appearance, but he quickly comforted those he visited and never tried to kill them. Muhammad's angel said that man was created from a blood clot. Genesis 2:7 states that man was created from the dust of the ground and that God breathed into him. This, along with other incompatibilities with the Torah and the Bible, demonstrate the angel was not Gabriel, the messenger of the Jewish and Christian God. Muhammad's wife was wrong which means he may have been right.

But why would a demon use the name Gabriel? Doesn't it seem like a bad imitation, like the spin off of an already successful movie? But the imitation is three-fold.

First, Lucifer, who is also Satan, said he wanted to be like God. (Isaiah 14:14) If God used Gabriel to announce the birth of Jesus and a revelation of the Kingdom on earth as an expansion of Judaism, then Satan would dress up a demon, name him Gabriel and send him to Muhammad to expand the religion of Al-Lat and Allah.

Second, using the name of an angelic being in the Bible establishes a common religious theme in the ancient world. Common is unexceptional. Skeptics see a shared belief among ancient religions, and they interpret such beliefs as made up. They say these created religions are spread by people practicing them and copied. Christian, Judaism and Islam are therefore equal.

Third, to those who believe the biblical Gabriel real, God sent new information to Muhammad to reveal His will for Islam. The name Gabriel is used to authenticate the message. As usual, Satan used imitation to deceive.

Paul warned of the religion of angels in Galatians 1:8-9, "But though we, or an angel from heaven, preach any other gospel unto you than that which we have preached unto you, let him be accursed. As we said before, so say I now again, If any man preach any other gospel unto you than that ye have received, let him be accursed."

It seems Muhammad was unsuccessful in abolishing the worship of Al-Lat over Allah. Many historians see common traditions in the modern Ka'bah in Mecca, the Black Stone and ancient Al-Lat religious ceremony. She is mentioned in the Qur'an.

Today Muslims believe that there are three revelations of God: Abraham, Jesus and Muhammad, of which Muhammad's Islam is the final revelation. His version is not the same as the book of Revelation in the Bible.

Muhammad was born over 400 years after the early Church began. He could have easily consulted a Christian about his "angelic" visitor. They most certainly set him right when he told them about his new philosophy. But his pride stopped him from believing the words spoken by those Christians and Jews he was hoping to impress.

Now that we know a little background about Islam's founding father, Muhammad, let's take a look at the religion and how it spread from Saudi Arabia into the northern reaches of the Middle East.

Muslims explain *jihad* as struggling or striving. They maintain it is not violent. The Islamic Supreme Council of America states that it has many meanings, including the ability to defend the faith. They insist it is not war against other religions and that the Qur'an urges respect for Christians and Jews.

They also claim there is a protocol that must be followed in jihad: women, children, and invalids should not be "harmed." The Council also states that "military action has not been common in the history of Islam."

However Muslims explain jihad, non-Muslims have a different experience with the concept. Jihad is related to the Arabic idea of attacking to defend. If for example the message of Islam is presented but rejected, the Muslim then has the right to defend his faith by attacking the person or governing body rejecting Islam.

David Wood states jihad exists in three steps visible from its beginnings to its present day identity. In the first part of jihad, Muslims who are outnumbered by the general population befriend non-Muslims, but portray themselves as victims in a society that restrains their beliefs. They voice peace but are planning their next move into step two as their populations increase.

In step two, their faith has been insulted, either intellectually, by physical limitations, or rejected individually or culturally. Note that criticism counts. In this portion of jihad, terror attacks are permitted and encouraged. This progresses into step three.

Step three is to declare war in order to purify the population and the land. Total subjugation is the goal. We can see this played out even in Muhammad's life in Mecca and Medina. We can also follow the steps as converts took their religion north.

The spread of Islam was met with resistance throughout the Middle East. Formerly, the regions had been a mix of polytheistic, Christian and Jewish communities. They had become part of the eastern portion of the Roman Empire which Constantine declared Christian in 330 AD.

Jordan was the first region Muhammad's followers took their new religion. By then the area was under Greek rule. But the Greeks lost their battle with the Muslims, and the Islamic Umayyad Caliphate ruled from Jordan, renaming the capitol Amman, the Arabic form of Ammon. Their power spread east to Pakistan and Uzbekistan.

As one region fell, Muslim soldiers went to the next. It resulted in the Arabization of the early Middle East's diverse cultures. Iran was invaded in 642 AD, but most Iranians were not Muslims until the sixteenth century. Even then, true success came when the religion was Persianized.

The same back and forth struggle ensued wherever the Islamists invaded. Turkey, Syria, Lebanon all battled for hundreds of years. (Remember, Israel did not exist as a country at this time. It had been taken over by various empires and its people scattered throughout the known world.)

There were four major Caliphs or reigning dynasties among other rival Caliphs. They were tolerant of other religions or not, depending on their interpretation of Islam. The Arabization of the cultures began to fade as other Islamic communities like the Iranian and Turkish cultures rose in power and influence.

Finally, the Ottoman Turks came to power and ruled a section of the world known as the Ottoman Empire. While the western part of Constantine's empire had fallen in 476, the eastern portion continued until the Muslim Turks won it in 1453. Their rule lasted 600 years. Jihad was a major tool in taking Islam to neighboring regions.

Contrary to what the Islamic Supreme Council states concerning the military actions of the Islamic religion, wars were common. Riad

M. Nasser, author of *Palestinian Identity in Jordan and Israel,* wrote (pg 100) that organizing to spread Islam decreased the fighting within the Muslim groups.

This is true to some extent. Of the first four leaders following Muhammad, three were assassinated. But military expeditions into neighboring regions unified the Muslims. Fighting others kept them from fighting amongst themselves– for a while. Caliphs continued to fight against each other for the right to rule their particular brand of Islam. Qur'an 109, 3:28.

Islam is not a Race

Some have accused people who speak against Islam as being racist. But technically Islam is a religion not a race. Today Muslims are people from ancient Canaanite, Egyptian, Persian, Babylonian and other groups of Indo European and Asiatic origins. In fact, they descend from every son of Noah.

The Middle East was a diverse group of people who were inundated with Arabic culture as the Arabic tribes swept into their communities. Muslims are converts, believers. A person is not born a Muslim and a person is not born a Christian. They are born into cultures with various skin, hair and eye colors. If a person carries DNA of Arabic or Persian ancestry, he can't change that. But he can change what he believes or what religion he is. A person born into a Muslim culture can decide to become another religion. (Not without persecution or possible death, of course. Refer to steps 1&2 of jihad.)

The problem with the word racist, however, is that some are using it to include motivation. This means that if you criticize Islam you are speaking from the same motivation as a person who hates a certain skin color. Australia's Parliament Member (and Muslim) Dr. Anne Aly is working to get Muslims included in the country's Racial Discrimination Act. But the fact remains, Islam is not a race.

Islam's Political Identity

Much is said about the separation of church and state in the United States. But true separation will never be accomplished because a society creates its governing body, its state, according to its values and what it believes to be true. Secularism, atheism, humanism and other belief systems that claim to be non-faith systems are, in practice, faith in man.

The portion of our Constitution that refers to the Separation of Church and State was included to insure that no faction of religion would become the supreme governing body. That is why we don't have the Baptist Party, the Methodist Party, etc. When John Kennedy was elected president, many feared his Catholic religion or the Pope would be the real ruler of the United States.

According to author, journalist and Lebanese Christian, Brigitte Gabriel, Muslims are not happy until they are in control. The modern history of Lebanon is an interesting study of Islam. Briefly, Lebanon came through the Muslim period and into the time period after WWI and WWII when France controlled it with more Christians than Muslims. This was a vastly different situation than most of the Middle Eastern region.

A government was established that required the president of Lebanon to be a Christian and the prime minister a Muslim. This remained the policy even after Lebanon gained its independence from France. Not until the 1960s did things begin to get complicated when Palestinian refugees started stirring the pot of discontent.

Lebanon was a country with open borders, as the term goes, and Yasser Arafat took advantage of it during his move to spread his followers into countries he thought needed purifying. At first the Palestinian presence was only in the south of Lebanon. It soon invaded northern towns and began killing Christians.

More Palestinians came, and soon the country was in a civil war. The Palestinians were not strong enough to resist a major army. But America ignored Lebanon's pleas for help. Syria's leader, Bashar Assad, saw his opportunity to take control and today Lebanon is not a functioning country. Modern Lebanon is paralyzed by Syria's dominance, now controlled by Iran and run by Hezbollah, a Shiite group that is Iran's proxy army. Do you see the stages of jihad in Lebanon's history?

According to a 2013 Pew Research study, in countries with Muslims as the majority, most favor adopting Islamic Law as the law that governs the country. There are liberal Muslims that don't want it and regular Muslims that don't and Muslims that favor it only in part– the part that doesn't require whippings and cutting off body parts. But these Muslims are not the majority.

The study is interesting as it reports that Muslims stated that non-Muslims can practice their religion freely. It also reports that they favor democracy. The more devout the Muslim, however, the more they want a religious leader involved in the government. That usually means Islamic Law.

Comparing the study with a list of the most dangerous places to be a Christian, one may wonder if some of the answers were honest. It is not true that Christians are able to practice their religion "freely" in a Muslim country. Government laws have made it illegal for a Muslim to convert to another religion, and in many Muslim countries the population of Christians is below 5%. Where it is higher, there are actions to eradicate it. Simply said, the only religion in a Muslim country that is completely legal and able to be exercised freely is Islam.

Thus, a truly Islamic country is currently incompatible with democracy (government ruled by the people). Even though a leader may be elected, the rule is strict obedience to the government (Islamic Law) at the expense of personal freedoms like choosing your own religion, style of dress or spouse. Turkey is tending toward this direction under its elected leader Erdogan.

It does seem that Brigitte Gabriel's statement "Muslims are only happy when they are in control" is accurate. It also seems that when they are in control other religions are not happy.

You may be wondering what a proxy army is, and just what is a Shiite?

The rivalry between the Sunni Muslims and the Shias or Shiites goes all the way back to Muhammad. After his death, no one knew who was supposed to be his successor. One group thought they should elect a righteous man; everyone should vote and the winner would be declared the leader. Those were the Sunnis.

The other group thought the leader should be a direct relative of Muhammad; leader by blood was their opinion. They were the Shias. The groups argued. Leaders were chosen over time and then assassinated one by one by the opposite party! The last straw came when a relative of Muhammad was killed, his family and children too. The groups have been enemies ever since.

There are various branches of these two groups. Currently Sunni countries outnumber Shiite ones. But, the Shiites are planning to change that. Iraq, Iran and Lebanon are countries where Shiites rule.

At times in history a Muslim leader has shown interest in westernizing his country. This means being more like the west in equality, dress, education, etc. Long before Erdogan, the present leader, westernization worked in Turkey. After WWI (the Ottoman Empire had been defeated in the war) Mustafa Kemal Atatürk, Turkey's leader, banned the caliph system and granted women rights. He organized the Republic of Turkey, and it was a success. Rezā Pahlavi, the Shah of Iran tried it, and it resulted in an Iranian Revolution (1979) that overthrew the monarchy and created a theocracy called the Islamic Republic of Iran. One clue to whose boss in Iran today– the Supreme Leader is an ayatollah, a Shiite religious leader.

The Shias and the Sunnis do not fight openly. Instead they support groups like Hezbollah, Hamas, Boko Haram, al Nusra, ISIS and others. ISIS and Hammas for example are Sunnis. So while Saudi Arabia may not have rolled out tanks, it has a military presence in various countries. The same is true for Iran and Turkey.

The groups, or proxy armies, are given money and provided with resources. For example, that is why Iran (Shia) is currently helping Syrian leader, Assad, a member of the Alawite branch of Shia, try to hang on to Syria and Lebanon. (The majority of Syria's population is Sunni, but they are ruled by the Shia.) Iran's motive is not charity, however. They want control.

It is complicated. One thing to remember is Genesis 16:12 says Ishmael will fight against all his brothers. And fight they do, drawing in other nations, affecting economies and creating refugee problems. Accusations fly between various groups because one is not seen as Muslim enough and therefore an offensive jihad commences to keep Islam and the land pure. This is why the power to rule is strong.

You might wonder what the average Muslim thinks of all this unrest. Many Muslims have never read the Qur'an in its entirety or the Hadith. Kind of like their Christian counterparts, they know certain verses in their holy books. But they have the same basic wants and needs as anyone else: security, a stable home and a way to support themselves. Terrorists governments put little emphasis on such needs. They are focused on jihad.

In 2010 young Muslims started uprisings that swept the Middle East. The uprisings were called the Arab Spring because it seemed to the world like a season of growth. It was a demand for democracy and better living conditions. Leaders in Egypt, Yemen, Libya and Tunisia were overthrown or killed. Protests were held in Saudi Arabia, Iraq, Jordan and other Muslim nations. But those young Arabs wanting freedoms were quickly overpowered by Islamic forces.

Instead of democracy, violence and terrorism has increased under the influence of jihadists. In 2017 and 2018 uprisings against Islamic leaders started again in Iran. Without international money provided by the nuclear deal, Iran may be in trouble.

The Future of Islam

Both Sunnis and Shias believe in the Mahdi. They differ, however, in his identity and origin. The Mahdi is an endtime figure thought of as the Muslim messiah who will come– or return depending on Sunni or Shiite claims– to establish peace and justice on earth. He reigns for seven years. Different versions of the prophecy say 5 years. Some say more than seven. He is only mentioned in the Hadith. Former Iranian president, Mahmoud Ahmadinejad, believed he and the Iranian government were chosen by Allah to hasten the Mahdi's appearance by creating chaos . Ahmadinejad prays for the Mahdi's return. He thinks the Mahdi will appear out of a well in the town of Jamkaran.

Both Sunnis and Shias believe the time of his coming is near. According to one version of Islam, Jesus will appear with the Mahdi, and the Mahdi will teach Him to pray. Others say the Mahdi will come first and Jesus later. Jesus will then promote the Qur'an, and all people in every nation will become Muslim. Islam will be the only and one true religion. Also, there will be no separation of church and state.

What we are willing to fight for is directly related to what we believe to be true and what we highly value. Islamic believers are encouraged to be martyrs for their religion, what they believe and highly value. It is the one way they are guaranteed salvation. It is not the one way of Christianity, the dependence on the blood and sacrifice of Jesus instead of ours and the death of others.

Ahmadinejad declared that the Mahdi will appear with blood and chaos. And that may be the truth, say those declaring the Mahdi is the anti-Christ of Revelation. Blood and chaos are the fruit of terrorism, and terrorism will continue to be a factor in the Middle East until Jesus returns. In the next chapter we'll learn what the Bible has to say about the future of the countries mentioned in the Bible.

• Chapter 5 •

Prophecies About the Middle East

Making predictions is sometimes like making an educated guess. The research states that practice improves your odds, at least in the realm of politics and business. It says experience and knowledge on your topic also improves your chances of being right. But that is not always the case. In recent elections in Israel and the United States, the majority of pollsters predicting election results were wrong.

Trying to predict money trends is just as tricky. Economic forecasters use computers to predict a range of possibilities. Not surprising due to their failure rate, but even with computers they failed to predict any of the recessions in 2008 and 2009. There were 62 world-wide. Oops.

How accurate is a groundhog in predicting the arrival of spring? Answer: 50% in the last 10 years.

Laugh if you want, but the humble groundhog has better luck than psychics. Their predictions, according to *The People's Almanac*, are 92% wrong. Many of their prophecies are generalized with very little detail which should help. But, no. Even the 8% right can be chalked up to common sense!

Business manager and author Peter Drucker said, "Trying to predict the future is like trying to drive down a country road at night with no lights while looking out the back window."

Apparently making accurate predictions is not easy. But when we speak of biblical prophecy, we are talking about predictions that were 100% accurate. No research or prior experience was required. No computer, groundhog or psychic either. Men (and women) from all walks of life, priests, judges, politicians, kings, shepherds and farmers, made accurate predictions. Average Joes and Janes.

The prophecies about Abraham's descendents like the one in Genesis 15:5? Fulfilled. The prophecies about Abraham's descendents having a country of their own? Fulfilled. The prophecies about the kingdom of Israel falling? Fulfilled. The prophecies about Israel becoming a nation again? Fulfilled. The promise in Leviticus 26:44 that God would never break His covenant with them? Fulfilled and being fulfilled.

And, drum roll please, the 300 plus prophecies foretelling Jesus' birth, death, resurrection and the meaning of all three? FULFILLED! Mathematics Professor Peter Stoner challenged his students to calculate the odds of one person fulfilling 300 prophecies. Their answer was that for one person to fulfill 16 prophecies the odds were 1 in 10^{45}. That's a lot of zeroes but only 16 prophecies. There are over 17 more sets of 16 to go!

The above prophecies deal only with Abraham, Israel and Jesus. Prophecies were also fulfilled that foretold the rise and fall of empires and their rulers. None of these prophesies were generalized predictions either. They were detailed. One thing we can learn from history and math class: the Bible can be trusted to make accurate predictions.

But there are biblical prophecies that haven't been fulfilled. These tell us what to expect in the "latter days."

Baker's Evangelical Dictionary of Biblical Theology provides a detailed definition of the term "latter days." Briefly, the Bible writers used the term to refer to the days after Jesus' death and resurrection. The apostles spoke of the time in which they lived as the last days. Peter testifies to this in Acts 2:16-17 and 1and 2 Peter. So no matter how long before Jesus returns, this is the age of the last days.

Another definition used is the end of days, or to make it more clear, the last of the last days, the time very close to Jesus' return. The latter portion of the last days was marked by many scholars as the time after Israel became a nation. In Matthew 24 the fig tree is Israel. This generation, Jesus said, is the generation that will see end events happen. Many biblical scholars and teachers believe this generation to be in place on the earth now. For a more detailed account of this read *Jesus Coming King: Are You Ready?*

If we are living in the last of the last days, how long before Jesus returns? Only God knows the exact time. But He has given us events to watch for that signal Jesus' return. These events involve Israel and its neighbors. The prophecies that are unfulfilled are those that pertain to Jesus' return.

So far we've studied the history, relationships and religious climate of the Middle East. Using that knowledge as our springboard, we can take a look at current world events and compare them with prophecies in the Bible that are to come. The major focus is the speck of earth containing the handful of cities in a spot the world calls the Holy Land, the land of the Bible.

Israel is in the news a lot concerning peace in the Middle East. Countries pressure Israel to agree to demands to give up land in order to create peace with the Palestinians. Israel is also pressed to give up rights to holy sites in favor of Muslim claims to them. This includes the site of Israel's First and Second Temple ruins, the Temple Mount. The only part remaining above ground is the wall connected to the Second Temple. It is called the Wailing Wall today.

Near the Wall, archaeologists are uncovering relics from the First Temple. The Dome of the Rock and the Al-Aqsa Mosque are built over the Temples' ruins. Muslims bulldozed the site to level it and scooped the debris into dump trucks to be unloaded on a hillside as trash. As you can imagine, the Temple Mount is a place of hostile controversy.

The holy site is a huge issue that unbelievers and casual believers have difficulty understanding. Holy sites have history. Reverence. Expectation. Remember our chapter on religion? Jews and Christians are expecting Jesus to return to Israel. The Muslims are expecting their Mahdi. He will reign for a time before Jesus returns to turn the whole world to Islam.

For years the Palestinians have claimed that Jewish ownership of a temple is a myth. King David? Didn't exist. The United Nations holds a similar view and the denial is growing in strength. Syrian-Lebanese author Joseph Farah asks the question, "How many Muslim holy sites are there in Israel?" None, he answers.

Since its birth, archaeology has uncovered evidence that backs up Farah's claim. Near the Temple Mount, Charles Warren discovered the original City of David in 1867. Since then, scores of finds have only supported Israel's right to the Temple Mount as ancient Jerusalem is being rebuilt.

Two of these finds are identical clay seals with the names Gedaliah ben Pashur on one and Yehuchal ben Shelemayahu on the other. They are 2,600 years old. Both men are mentioned in Jeremiah 38:1 as being ministers of King Zedekiah. He was the last king before the First Temple was destroyed.

Recently the 2,000 year old road leading from the City of David up to the Temple Mount during the Second Temple period was discovered. At the site of ancient Lachish, an important trade city larger than Jerusalem at the time, the Israeli flag now flies over the spot Assyria waged a war. Assyrian records found in Ninevah give us details, but the mound in Israel has revealed a ramp built to scale Lachish's outer wall, round stones for slingshots, arrowheads and caves used as death pits for beheaded Hebrews.

The Shiloah Project inscription is 2,700 years old. King Hezekiah's seal about the same. 3,000 year old plus finds are found at the ruins of Shiloh, Ela, Gezer and David's Spring Citadel. Numerous ancient wells, tunnels, roads, inscriptions, coins, etc. all give testimony to the rulers, culture and Israeli possession of the land long before many of the countries in the United Nations existed. Holy sites included. The conclusion is simple: if you want to know about the ancient Israelites go to what is called the Holy Land, that part of Canaan they conquered and ruled.

For those who support Israel's existence, to deny Israel possessed, lived in and remained in the land is like saying the Egyptians have no right to Egypt even though scores of artifacts and pyramids say otherwise. In the United States, the comparison might be made to Native American tribes who we know possessed, lived in and remained in the land despite being conquered and scattered. But most people in the States recognize their right to at least a parcel of their homeland, holy sites and a tribal government. The largest Native American Reservation in the United States is 27,096 square miles. In total, 56 million acres are held in trust on behalf of Indian tribes.

In contrast, Israel is only 8,019 square miles which is around 5 million acres and many do not want them to have possession of that.

Muslims say that Muhammad made a physical and spiritual journey from Mecca to the Temple in Jerusalem (S. 17:1). The problem is the Second Temple was destroyed in 70AD, hundreds of years before Muhammad's visit. No mosque was there either. According to Sam Shamoun, the Arabic word, *masjid*, can refer to a place to pray, but in this verse it means building. It is *al-Masji al-Aqsa*, a word used only for the *Jewish* Temple. In light of these facts, Muslim holy books do not provide an accurate account of this proposed journey.

But the Israelis' claim to the region is evident using multiple sources: the Christian Bible, the Torah, history and archaeology. Gen 17:8 says, "And I will give unto thee, and to thy seed after thee, the land wherein thou art a stranger, all the land of Canaan, for an everlasting possession; and I will be their God." Notice that God said all the land of Canaan, and He considers it theirs forever. It is an area described larger than their current borders. This includes the Temple Mount and all of Jerusalem.

Everyday Jews pray for a Third Temple to be built. Plans for it are on display in a Hebrew museum. Revelation 11:2 describes a temple so it seems a Third Temple will be constructed at some time in the future.

The United States' recognition of Jerusalem as the capital of Israel has encouraged Temple supporters. Animal sacrifices have also been made in recent years. In 2015 a lamb was sacrificed 4 kilometers from the Temple Mount. In 2016, 1.5 kilometers away. In April 2017 400 meters. In 2018, 10 meters from the Temple. One day the ceremony will take place in a Third Temple.

One fact the world seems to ignore or miss is that to Israel all of the land is a holy site. We've already learned God's borders for Israel do not please Muslims. But while all the land of Israel is controversial to Muslims, the West Bank is the most misunderstood by the world.

It is conveniently called the West Bank, but its real name is Judea and Samaria, and Israel has the right to all of the land along the west bank of the Jordan River. They can even claim land along the eastern bank in southern Jordan, part of Syria and Lebanon.

In the *Mandate for Palestine*, Israel was guaranteed land encompassing modern Israel plus Judea, Samaria (the West Bank), Gaza, Jordan and a section in northwest Saudi Arabia. The League of Nations agreed with the ruling July 24, 1922. The document is still legally in effect.

Administrations after 1922 delayed enacting the agreement because they were trying to appease the Arabs. Remember Emir Abdullah? By 1947, Britain surrendered their role in the *Mandate*. It was then left to others to solve the Arab problem. It's never been solved.

Israel's leaders have surrendered more land for peace in recent years. But land for peace has never satisfied the Palestinians, Jordanians or any other country surrounding Israel. Only the Jews' complete annihilation would stop the bickering. Until they started fighting with each other— Shia and Sunni.

Israelis are referred to as *occupying the West Bank* which includes the town of Bethlehem. God is not pleased with those words. Israelis are not occupiers but rightful heirs to their eternal home. And, that eternal home will be restored to them when Jesus returns, and it will be larger than what they presently own.

The problem is Muslim's do not recognize the Bible, the Torah or the one God of both books as their authority. But their Qur'an advises them to. Remember when Muhammad was first starting out and he confirmed the Bible and the Torah? Later he changed his mind. However, in 3.3 the Qur'an still affirms the Bible and the Torah as the revelation of Allah. It says his words cannot be changed (6.115).

The Bible message has never changed throughout its existence. Think of all it declares. Muslims are pledged to honor it by their own writings from Allah? While Arabic Muslims claim Abraham as their flesh ancestor too, which is correct, they distort the actual history and agreement between Abraham and God. God agreed to bless Ishmael's family, gave them land too, but did not give any of his sons the land He gave to Israel. Abraham, their own father, "sent them away" from his other son Isaac. (Genesis 25:6)

Abraham built three altars in what is now the West Bank at Hebron, Shechem (modern Nablus) and Bethel. Joshua gathered the tribes at Shechem, Joseph's Tomb is there and Abimelech (Judges) was crowned king there. Abraham offered Isaac to God on Mt. Moriah which is the location of the Temple Mount and the Dome of the Rock. Joshua established an altar in Shiloh, also in the West Bank, where the Tabernacle (Tent of Meeting) stood. Moses received the Ten Commandments in Midian (Saudi Arabia north of Mecca) and the nation of Israel was organized there.

All these sites are currently claimed by Arabic Muslims. The problem is not Arabs; the problem is Islam and its doctrines. Isaiah 14:13 explains that Satan wants to exalt himself above all that is God's. "For thou hast said in thine heart, I will ascend into heaven, I will exalt my throne above the stars of God: I will sit also upon the mount of the congregation..." Islam is an anti-Judeo-Christian and anti-Semitic message. But Isaiah goes on to say, "Yet thou shalt be brought down to hell, to the sides of the pit." (Isaiah 14:15) This spiritual conflict about holy sites is the source of the earthly conflict in the Middle East and spills over to the rest of the world.

Ezekiel records a prophecy given to him while he was a captive in Babylon. He was to speak two messages to the mountains of Israel, actually the West Bank today. The condensed version is Israel is going to get their holy places back, and the nations who took them and said, "Ahah! We got 'em!" are going to pay. Here is a portion of the message to the guilty nations:

> Thus saith the Lord GOD; Because the enemy hath said against you, Aha, even the ancient high places are ours in possession: Therefore prophesy and say, Thus saith the Lord GOD; Because they have made you desolate, and swallowed you up on every side, that ye might be a possession unto the residue of the heathen, and ye are taken up in the lips of talkers, and are an infamy of the people: Therefore, ye mountains of Israel, hear the word of the Lord GOD; Thus saith the Lord GOD to the mountains, and to the hills, to the rivers, and to the valleys, to the desolate wastes, and to the cities that are forsaken, which became a prey and derision to the residue of the heathen that are round about; Therefore thus saith the Lord GOD; Surely in the fire of my jealousy have I spoken against the residue of the heathen, and against all Idumea[Edom], which have appointed my land into their possession with the joy of all their heart, with despiteful minds, to cast it out for a prey. Prophesy therefore concerning the land of Israel, and say unto the mountains, and to the hills, to the rivers, and to the valleys, Thus saith the Lord GOD; Behold, I have spoken in my jealousy and in my fury, because ye have borne the shame of the heathen: Therefore thus saith the Lord GOD; I have lifted up mine hand,

> Surely the heathen that are about you, they shall bear their shame. (Ezekiel 36:2-7)

Palestinians are demonstrating in London and Israel concerning their right to land given to Israel in 1948. But as God has decreed, Israel will not be going away soon. The city of Akka on Israel's northeast coast is a place where the people seem to have accepted that fact. Jews, Muslims and Christians live and worship alongside each other peacefully.

Nevertheless, anti-Semitism is on the rise everywhere else. Concerning prejudice and hostility toward Jews, CNN reported that the rate of incidents rose 86% higher in the first three months of 2017 than the previous year. In England, *The Independent* ran an article that stated 767 incidents were reported in the first six months of 2017. These statistics are dramatic, but a steady increase has been seen in the last few years.

Another trending item of concern is the persecution of Christians. Fox News reported that 90,000 Christians were killed for their faith or because of the label each year for the last ten years. Or, 1 every 6 minutes. These are numbers not seen since Roman times. The report went on to say that Christians are 1/3 of the world's population, but 2/3 of that number live in dangerous places where Christianity is not "as easy as it is in America or Europe."

But how easy is it in Europe to practice your faith? Catholic Bishop Manfred Scheuer says not very. Lutheran Bishop Hans-Jörg Voigt states that Germany is refusing to grant asylum to former Muslims who become Christians. To deport them means their torture and death. According to Pope Francis, there are more martyrs world-wide today than in the early days of the Church. These statistics make Christianity the most persecuted religion in the world.

The same studies report the majority of top ten countries where persecution is prevalent are Muslim. The climate seems to be growing more dangerous for those worshipping and believing in the God of the Bible. Jesus outlined the events leading up to His return in Mark 13 and a surge in persecution is on the list as the time draws nearer.

ISIS is responsible for beheading, crucifying and brutally murdering Christians. In fact, *Fox News* featured a video released by ISIS stating, "Christians are their favorite prey." ISIS is responsible for displacing over 1 million Iraqis and millions more in Syria, Lebanon, Turkey and Yemen. Kurds are the latest target, and a new enemy is emerging: Turkey.

President Recep Tayyip Erdogan is buying long range missiles from Russia. Remember his plans to resurrect the Ottoman Empire? From 1913 to 1922 the Ottoman Empire/Turkey was responsible for killing over a million Christian Armenians and Greeks. Its rulers, including Mustafa Kemal Atatürk, were on a mission to cleanse the country. Turkey for Turks, they said. It is illegal to talk about it in Turkey today.

Earlier in the 1890s, thousands more were killed. Jews as well. Is this what we can expect from a new Ottoman Empire? Erdogan is promoting Turkish nationalism (patriotism and superiority), and says that Christians and Jews are enemies of the state. But he doesn't like them outside of Turkey either.

Years ago Middle East expert, Avi Lipkin said that the world is marching toward an Elijah moment. He was referring to Elijah's showdown with the prophets of Baal. A showdown is exactly what the Bible predicts.

Even with the persecutions and unrest, we are witnessing only a portion of what is to come for people of God in the Middle East. Mark 13:19-20 says, "For in those days shall be affliction, such as was not from the beginning of the creation which God created unto this time, neither shall be. And except that the Lord had shortened those days, no flesh should be saved: but for the elect's sake, whom he hath chosen, he hath shortened the days."

Biblical prophecy focuses on the Middle East. There are references to European empires and rulers, but the majority of prophecy centers around Israel, more specifically Jerusalem. It is from the New Jerusalem that Jesus will rule. What we see in today's headlines concerning the fight over Jerusalem is a visual sign of a spiritual battle. That spiritual battle will increase as the end times unfold and Satan gives all he's got to win complete control.

What we've discussed so far about the conflicts over land and religion might seem redundant. But it is the back and forth struggle of a battle we only see in part. As we near the end of the end of days, this conflict will escalate and accelerate.

Of all endtime prophecies, there is only one battle scholars seem to agree on. It is the battle recorded in Ezekiel 38 known by many as the first Gog Magog war.

Ezekiel 38 and 39 are two of the most puzzling chapters of Bible prophecy. Scholars debate the identity of Gog and Magog mentioned in the text, but knowing who they are is crucial to understanding the message. There are a few lines of thought concerning them. Gog may be a ruler named Gagu in Assyrian records or the cruel Lydian ruler named Gugu. It could be a name for Babylon or a general title used for a king. Some think it is a reference to the ruler (Gog) and the land (Magog) of Russia.

There is an interesting twist in the idea of identifying Gog with Babylon, however. It seems Ezekiel may know the ruler and the land. Ezekiel 38:2 says, "…set thy face against Gog, the land of Magog, the chief prince of Meshech and Tubal, and prophesy against him."

Ezekiel was in Babylon. Nebuchadnezzar's father had conquered the Assyrian Empire by making friends with the Medes and Scythians so that they would help him. He finalized the deal by marrying off his son to the Median king's daughter. This would allow the son, Nebuchadnezzar, to be the prince Ezekiel is referring to as he was the acting prince of the land of the Scythians and Medes which included Togarmah, Gomer, Tubal and Meshech.

Notice that the verse says *prophecy against him*. Another theory is Gog is the unseen demonic ruler over the region. Paul tells us that there are rulers and principalities in the heavens. (Ephesians 2:2, 3:10 and 6:12) The theories actually combine to form a good picture. A ruler of a nation from the north will act at the prompting, knowingly or unknowingly, of a ruling demonic power to unite other countries against Israel. All of the people represented in the verse lived in the region north and northeast of Iraq.

The principle of a demonic ruler acting through an earthly ruler is also presented in Ezekiel's prophecy against Tyre. In Ezekiel 28 he continues to speak against Tyre which was a powerful fortified, rich city in the ancient world. It was built on a rock island off the coast of Lebanon. In the beginning, Ezekiel is addressing the king who thought of himself as a god. But Ezekiel reminds him that he is only a man.

By verse 12 Ezekiel is addressing another king of Tyre who had been in the Garden of Eden. This is Satan, and we gain insight into what he was before he became the adversary and why he became one. The important thing for our focus is that Satan was named as the king or ruler of Tyre in the spiritual realm over it. In Ezekiel 28 we learn an earthly king is naming himself a god under the influence and power emanating down from the unseen principality above him.

Jesus in Revelation 2:12-13 says to the church in Pergamum, "And to the angel of the church in Pergamos write; These things saith he which hath the sharp sword with two edges; I know thy works, and where thou dwellest, even where Satan's seat is." Apparently Satan moves his operations from time to time.

Pergamos was an important city in Asia Minor (Turkey) that rivaled Athens during the Roman Empire. But it was dark. The people considered themselves "temple keepers." There was the temple for the emperor, for Athena and the Altar of Zeus. Scholars like Rick Renner believe Zeus's altar was the throne of Satan. Renner says that the word throne was first used to identify the seat for the master or lord of the house. Jesus, by using the word throne, was saying Satan felt at home there, like Dad or Grandpa in their favorite chair.

But then along came a Christian pastor named Antipas, and the priests of the local snake healing cult complained that demons had told them in their dreams that Antipas' prayers were driving them out of the city. Antipas was bound and put into the statue of a bronze bull used for human sacrifices on the altar of Zeus. A fire was lit under the bull. Antipas' cries, during a painful death, seemed to make the bull come alive. The rest of Revelation 2:13 states, "and thou holdest fast my name, and hast not denied my faith, even in those days wherein Antipas was my faithful martyr, who was slain among you, where Satan dwelleth."

Hundreds of years later, the altar was brought to Berlin, Germany and reconstructed in 1930 just in time for it to inspire Adolph Hitler. A replica of the altar was built. In Nuremburg, religious like ceremonies featured his Messiah type entrance and lights imitating God's glory and themes of the Catholic Church. It was also from this replica on a platform in place of the bull that Hitler announced his plans for the Holocaust, a burnt sacrifice. This time for Jews. Coincidence? Probably not.

It will be the same during the two Gog Magog wars of the latter days. A demonic ruler will be influencing the earthly ruler(s). His seat of power will be north of Israel. Daniel 8:23-25 says:

> And in the latter time of their kingdom, when the transgressors are come to the full, a king of fierce countenance, and understanding dark sentences, shall stand up. And his power shall be mighty, but not by his own power: and he shall destroy wonderfully, and shall prosper, and practice, and shall destroy the mighty and the holy people. And through his policy also he shall cause craft to prosper in his hand; and he shall magnify himself in his heart, and by peace shall destroy many: he shall also stand up against the Prince of princes; but he shall be broken without hand.

Ezekiel 38 and 39 tell about this future battle between Gog, Magog and their allies. The allies are listed as Persia, Put, Cush, Gomer, Togarmah, Meshech and Tubal. These are the modern day names associated with these regions in order: Iran, Libya, Ethiopia, Turkey, Armenia, Russia, Azerbaijan and western Asia. Iraq is represented possibly by Gog. Ezekiel 38:6 and 15 also include the statement that they come from the "uttermost parts of the north." (ASV) This large army will gather on Israel's border. (It is of note that the majority of these countries, or parts of them were in the Ottoman Empire.)

Ezekiel 38:13 mentions Sheba, Dedan and the merchants of Tarshish asking these countries "Art thou come to take a spoil?... to carry away silver and gold?... to take a great spoil?" Not that these countries, who are Yemen, Saudi Arabia, Syria and Lebanon, want to protect Israel. They will probably want some of the spoil.

But why are they not allied with those attacking Israel? The question was puzzling until now. Lebanon and Syria are no longer functioning countries. They are run by Iran's proxy Shia armies and propped up by both Iran and Russia. Now Turkey wants in on the prize. Yemen is in the process of being taken over by Iranian backed Shia forces. ISIS and al-Qaeda are gaining ground at Saudi Arabia's door. Millions of people, including children, are dying in another Shia vs. Sunni civil war. So far Saudi forces (Sunni) have not been successful in eradicating the Shias.

Prophecy scholars are watching current headlines with interest because this alliance of Gog and Magog is smiling back at them from screens and newsprint. A picture of the rulers of Iran, Turkey and Russia gathered to decide the fate of Syria signaled an alliance not quite like others of the past. Plans to unite an Islamic army from fifty-seven nations (Organization of Islamic Cooperation) to attack Israel were reported in a Turkish newspaper in 2018.

Erdogan's desire to bring back the Ottoman Empire may be Satan's attempt to imitate God's resurrection of Israel. Whatever Erdogan's goals, Saudi Arabia has reasons to fear this rising caliphate because the Shias want to control Mecca and Medina. The Saudis are not able to defend themselves and are reaching out to Israel for help. The populations of Yemen, Syria and Lebanon are also powerless to resist Iran, Russia and Turkey. These facts may shed light on the above verse asking Gog about his army. These countries are not in positions to lead.

Another interesting detail happened in October of 2015. It was announced that vast oil reserves were discovered in the Golan Heights in Israel near the Syrian border. And, already swarming Israel's northern border are enemies like Hezbollah, Hamas and ISIS groups, made up of soldiers from various countries surrounding Israel. Turkey and

Russia are also lurking nearby. A Pew Research study found that the countries surrounding Israel held low percentages concerning Jewish favorability. All were under 5%; the majority under 4%. This probably doesn't surprise you at this point.

In the illustration below, Israel is represented as the solid black sliver among the surrounding Muslim countries shaded in gray.

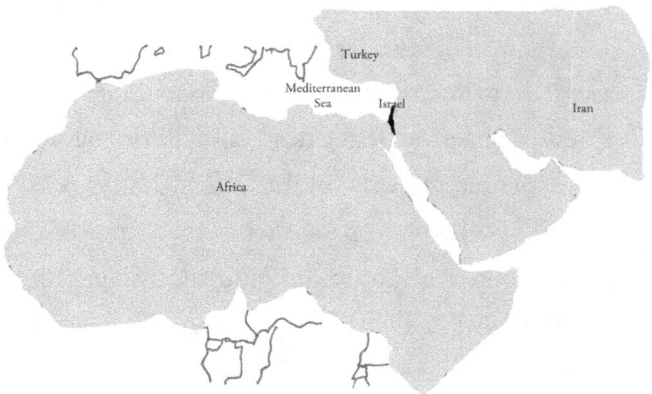

So there is the tension in the Middle East as we have learned about since chapter one, but now Gog and Magog are present, and strife seems to be increasing for many reasons— holy sites/land, religion and oil. The situation may morph into something biblical or it could fade away as history being made.

That something biblical is Ezekiel's war. To Israel God gives the warning that when He brings them back to their country, after it had been lost to war, in a time when no walls are built around their cities, an enemy will come to them. Therefore they must be watchful so they can protect their people. So far they have done this pretty well.

> Gomer, and all his bands; the house of Togarmah of the north quarters, and all his bands: and many people with thee. Be thou prepared, and prepare for

> thyself, thou, and all thy company that are assembled unto thee, and be thou a guard unto them. After many days thou shalt be visited: in the latter years thou shalt come into the land that is brought back from the sword, and is gathered out of many people, against the mountains of Israel, which have been always waste: but it is brought forth out of the nations, and they shall dwell safely all of them. Thou shalt ascend and come like a storm, thou shalt be like a cloud to cover the land, thou, and all thy bands, and many people with thee. Thus saith the Lord GOD; It shall also come to pass, that at the same time shall things come into thy mind, and thou shalt think an evil thought: And thou shalt say, I will go up to the land of unwalled villages; I will go to them that are at rest, that dwell safely, all of them dwelling without walls, and having neither bars nor gates, To take a spoil, and to take a prey; to turn thine hand upon the desolate places that are now inhabited, and upon the people that are gathered out of the nations, which have gotten cattle and goods, that dwell in the midst of the land. (Ezekiel 38:6-12)

Then a huge army representing the countries mentioned earlier will gather to annihilate Israel. God says about the army, "Thou shalt ascend and come like a storm, thou shalt be like a cloud to cover the land, thou, and all thy bands, and many people with thee." (Ezekiel 38:9) It may be an aerial attack or missiles or even chemicals that "shall be like a cloud." But they are not successful.

Ezekiel prophesied that God, in a supernatural act, will protect Israel from this army. A massive earthquake will happen, a plague will break out, and the enemy will start killing each other. Torrential rainstorms with hailstones will begin, fire and brimstone will fall on them, and then everyone will know that God is in charge. It will be a newsworthy event. Israel will be cleaning up the carnage for seven years!

In the Yad Ben-Zvi Institute in Jerusalem there are sixty-six plates inscribed in Hebrew. They were discovered in Ezekiel's Tomb in Iraq. On them is written the book of Ezekiel and the plates may be the original writings. If the plates survive the calamity, one day what is considered archaeology will be like reading modern day headlines.

Some scholars link this battle with the one in Revelations 20:7-10. Others argue that is the second war between Israel and again Gog and Magog. One theory is that there are three wars in Revelation. The Ezekiel war just described, possibly reflected in Revelation 6 during the sixth seal, one at Jesus' return where He fights Satan's army and Satan is locked up for a thousand years, and another Gog Magog war after Satan is let loose for the last time and is again defeated in Revelation 20:7-10.

But there are at least two, and Ezekiel's war is definitely one of them. Which, and just how far we are in God's timetable of end time events, is still debated. End time scholars who support the three war theory point out that Ezekiel does not mention an anti-Christ man as a supreme leader of the region in the first war like the one described in Revelation. Also, Jesus does not fight in this first battle, they say. In the war in Revelation 20 and Zechariah 14, however, Jesus and His heavenly army fight against an anti-Christ leader and his earthly army.

Ezekiel repeats a theme for this first war. It is this: " ...that the heathen may know me, when I shall be sanctified in thee, O Gog, before their eyes." (Ezekiel 38:16) God concludes the war by saying, "Thus will I magnify myself, and sanctify myself; and I will be known in the eyes of many nations, and they shall know that I am the LORD." (Ezekiel 38:23)

It seems this war will have an evangelistic end, and hopefully many will convert to Christianity. The miraculous aspect of this war will be undeniable. And, it could happen at anytime under the present circumstances. You can read more in our book, *Ezekiel The Prophet: Why His Message Matters To Us*.

The book of Revelation tells the story of what will happen in the last days from heaven's viewpoint. The Apostle John is telling the story while he is standing in heaven in his vision. Daniel also had a vision of what will happen in the last days. It is recorded in Daniel 11 and 12. Revelation and Daniel agree that an army will come from the north to invade Israel and steal its hidden treasure while hoping to annihilate the country. That hidden treasure might be the recently discovered oil. It will probably be an earthly goal for both Gog Magog wars. The spiritual goal in both will be to eliminate Christians and Jews.

The person leading the anti Christ army in Revelation 11 and 17 will be a man who will rise out of the old Roman Empire's territory to take over the Middle East. Could it be Asia Minor, Turkey, one of the former seats of Satan? Is that why the seven churches in Revelations are all in Turkey? Or is he the leader of the European Union? The world may soon find out. But the ancient regions of Edom, Moab and Ammon, which is Jordan, will escape his grasp. Some Israelites will flee to Jordan.

This man is referred to as the anti-Christ. The apostle John warned that many anti-Christs will appear in the world and some were on the earth in his day. He defined an anti-Christ as one who denies Jesus came as God in the flesh. But this man who will battle Jesus in the

Revelation war is the major anti-Christ. Think of what that means. We have already experienced brutal, murderous dictators. This one will outrank them all. But his rule is short. Three and a half years.

Revelation speaks of a scroll sealed with seven seals. There are similarities between the events listed in the scrolls and Jesus' words about the end times in Matthew 24, signs in the sky, persecution and war.

But there are other prophecies besides the Gog Magog war. Revelation 11 describes a Jerusalem we have not seen yet. It may be ruled by the man called the anti-Christ. It is described as Sodom and Egypt it is so wicked. It won't allow two of God's witnesses to be buried, but gloats over their murder at the hands of the man called the anti-Christ. A revival of sorts will take place after the two witnesses come back to life after three days and an earthquake rocks the city.

Babylon is referred to in Revelation, but some scholars believe it is symbolic of the source of all idolatry and persecutions in history rather than representing the country of Iraq. Babylon whether a real city at the time of this event or not is where demons live. (Revelations 18:2) It is the site where Nimrod established false religion and perhaps the reason Gog, the demonic ruler, is said to reign there. It is the theological source of every religion outside of Judaism and Christianity.

Biblical prophecies sometimes have near, far and far-far components. They can be partially fulfilled with the complete and perfect fulfillment occurring later. For example, Daniel predicted a temple's destruction and desecration in Daniel 11. But there was no temple because Babylon had destroyed the First Temple. Later, King Cyrus of the Persian Empire helped the Jews build a Second Temple when he allowed them to return to their land as told in Ezra and Nehemiah.

Hundreds of years later in 167 BC, Antiochus Epiphanes, a ruler of the Greek influenced empire in Persia, killed 40,000 Jews. Another

40,000 were sold as slaves. He set up an altar to Zeus in the Temple in Jerusalem and sacrificed pigs. Later the Temple was rededicated by the Jews and Jewish worship was reinstated. The building was improved and expanded under Herod the Great during the lifetime of Jesus and shortly after.

Finally, Titus destroyed the Second Temple in 70 AD on the 9th of Av, the same day Nebuchadnezzar had destroyed the First Temple. Titus invited Jews to enter the city and then captured them. They died of starvation. Hadrian reneged on his efforts to rebuild a Jewish Temple, dedicating it to Zeus instead.

A Muslim site sits over the Temple today. It seems the prophecy has been fulfilled, a few times. But a closer look of Daniel's prophecy reveals another Temple and destruction to come. Daily sacrifices are being offered then forced to stop in Revelation 11. That is probably happening in a Third Temple which hasn't been built yet but will be.

Three and a half years will pass and the "desolation" will be set up. No one is sure what the desolation is, but it will be something that defiles the Temple like before under the Babylonians and Romans. Also, the anti-Christ who establishes this desolation will die in Israel. That hasn't happened yet. (Antiochus Epiphanes died in Iran. Titus and Hadrian died in Italy.) Similar circumstances have happened, but the complete prophecy will be fulfilled at a future time.

All the nations of the Middle East will be judged according to their treatment of Israel. At the end of days in the final chapters of Revelation they will have to bow to God and confess that Jesus is Lord. The fact will be beyond dispute. Israel will be reunited with God, spiritually and physically. There will still be people and nations on the earth during the thousand year reign of Christ. These nations will come to worship in Jerusalem where King David will rule. Some think it is really

King David; others think it means Jesus because He is a descendant of David. There will be two Jerusalems that unite, the heavenly Jerusalem that will descend from the sky and the one on the earth.

One other prophecy that is not restricted to the Middle East is that of the rapture or the catching away of believers. One day, suddenly, in the twinkling of an eye, thousands of people will disappear. This seems to be related to Ezekiel's first war but could happen at any time. For more details of the rapture and end time events that Zechariah and other prophets predicted, read *Jesus Coming King: Are You Ready?*

How can we be certain these events will happen? Besides the 2,000 prophecies already accurately fulfilled, ten prophecies concerning Israel have been fulfilled since 1948. We may be witnessing other prophecies being fulfilled concerning Ezekiel 38 right now. That is why many Christians and Jews are calling our days Bible Times. But ordinary people may not recognize these events as anything other than the news. Jesus said it will be like the days of Noah.

> But as the days of Noe were, so shall also the coming of the Son of man be. For as in the days that were before the flood they were eating and drinking, marrying and giving in marriage, until the day that Noe entered into the ark, And knew not until the flood came, and took them all away; so shall also the coming of the Son of man be. (Matthew 24:37-39)

This may mean that the trouble is centered in the Middle East, as usual, with the rest of the world affected, but remote. They will hear about the goings on, but have no idea what they mean. In fact, the circumstances may seem ordinary for the region, able to be explained. Then, seemingly all at once, disaster strikes and people disappear.

Jesus, Peter, John and Paul talked about what will happen to believers in the end times. Amid the persecutions, a great revival will happen. Maybe this will happen after the events in Ezekiel 38 or during what is called the tribulation, the reign of the anti-Christ. Probably both. In part it is happening today. Despite the dangers, more Muslims are coming to Jesus than ever before.

These are the prophecies concerning the Middle East. To sum up, we are looking for a temple to be built sometime in Israel, a man to rise out of the former Roman Empire to control the Middle East by influence or might who hates Jews and Christians and who unites a huge army to fight Israel. There may be one Gog Magog war or two, instigated by a country north of Israel. The war will be led by Turkey or Russia or financed by them. But they will be defeated by miraculous circumstances.

After that, Israel will clean up the mess. If the Third Temple is not built and controlled in the first war, then it will be controlled in the next. Israel will eventually regain its land and more; Jerusalem will be its capital and all nations will go there to worship because all nations will honor the God of the Torah and the Bible.

There is an element of time to these first events, but if Revelation is understood just as it is written, the very last days will be a seven year period. The situation escalates when the major anti-Christ man takes control. The future for all nations in the world boils down to their choice to support Israel or not. If they do not, destruction and punishment await. Even so, countries boldly stand against Israel regularly.

Besides the disastrous Iranian Nuke Deal, one example happened on December 23, 2016. The United Nations Security Council Resolution #2334 passed 14-0. The Resolution declared Jewish people living in the Jewish Quarter of the Old City of Jerusalem are illegal occupants. Further, it said Jews could not pray at their holy sites. December 23, 2016, was Hanukkah, the Jewish holiday that celebrates Judah the Maccabee's victory in liberating the Second Temple from the Greeks. The date seemed to be chosen for its significance.

America chose to abstain, but it could have voted against it. Instead it allowed the resolution to pass. Silence equaled a yes. Fourteen countries and America voted against Israel.

Things have changed in America under a different President and the discovery of the Palestinian Pay-To-Slay campaign. Still, most nations' rulers do not even consider what the Bible says. Jesus said that many would be deceived, and love toward God would grow cold. These countries will not be ready when Jesus returns. They will be absorbed in their activities and pay no attention to the signs God gives in the sun, moon and stars and the events happening around them and through them.

Jesus said the wise will know when the time is near and will be watching. He said to pray to be able to escape the turmoil to come upon the earth. The church in Philadelphia was commended for their diligence in the things of God, and they were promised God's deliverance from the trial which will come to the whole earth. (Revelation 3:10)

Daniel also said the wise will know. Paul wrote, "But of the times and the seasons, brethren, ye have no need that I write unto you. For yourselves know perfectly that the day of the Lord so cometh as a thief in the night. For when they shall say, Peace and safety; then sudden destruction cometh upon them, as travail upon a woman with child; and they shall not escape. But ye, brethren, are not in darkness, that that day should overtake you as a thief. Ye are all the children of light, and the children of the day: we are not of the night, nor of darkness." (1 Thessalonians 5:1-5)

Do you know how many understood the times when Jesus' was born, when He came the first time? How many were watching? How many read the prophecies and calculated His birth? How many paid attention to or understood the signs in the sky? Not Herod. Not the Emperor of Rome. Not the ordinary people or the believers.

The answer is one old man and one old woman in a synagogue and a handful of men from the East. (Only by an invitation did the shepherds witness it.) And what were the men from the East called? Wise men.

Thank you for purchasing *Countries in the Bible: Who They Are Today*. We hope this book helps you understand the Bible and current news events better. If you enjoyed reading it, please consider leaving a review where you discovered the book or email us. Check out other titles at flyingeaglepublications.com or sign up for our email list and receive articles from the blog, freebies and news. You can also follow us on Facebook.

Bibliography

Chapter 1 Countries in the Bible
Associated Press. "Mosul struggles to rebuild in wake of ISIS destruction." *New York Post,* December 28, 2017, https://nypost.com/2017/12/28/mosul-struggles-to-rebuild-in-wake-of-isis-destruction/

"Beautiful Babylon: Jewel of the Ancient World." *History Magazine,* https://www.nationalgeographic.com/archaeology-and-history/magazine/2017/01-02/babylon-mesopotamia-ancient-city-iraq/

Berkowitz, Adam Eliyahu. "Biblical Origins of the 70-Nation Anti-Israel Paris Conference." *Breaking Israel News,* January 5, 2017, https://www.breakingisraelnews.com/81577/return-70-nations-paris-condemn-israel/#Ifs66jxtKuvvG5Bw.97

Byers, Gary. "The Biblical Cities of Tyre and Sidon." *Bible and Spade Fall 2002, Associates for Biblical Research,* Posted January 26, 2010, http://www.biblearchaeology.org/post/2010/01/26/The-Biblical-Cities-Of-Tyre-And-Sidon.aspx#Article

Curry, Andrew. "World's Oldest Temple Restored." *National Geographic,* January 20, 2016, https://news.nationalgeographic.com/2016/01/150120-gobekli-tepe-oldest-monument-turkey-archaeology/

Exploring Jordan The Other Biblical Land. Bible Archaeology Society, 2008. E-book
Fausset, A. R. (1949) *Fausset's Bible Dictionary*. Grand Rapids, Michigan: Zondervan.

Garcia, Brittany. "Ishtar Gate." *Ancient History Encyclopedia,* August 23, 2013, https://www.ancient.eu/Ishtar_G

Habermehl, Anne. "Where in the World Is the Tower of Babel?" *Answers in Genesis,* March 23, 2011, https://answersingenesis.org/tower-of-babel/where-in-the-world-is-the-tower-of-babel/

Haughton, Brian. "Haughton Gobekli Tepe - the World's First Temple?" *Ancient History Encyclopedia,* May 4, 2011 https://www.ancient.eu/article/234/gobekli-tepe--the-worlds-first-temple/

"Himyarite Dynasty of Yemen." *Amazing Bible Timeline,* https://amazingbibletimeline.com/blog/himyarite-dynasty-of-yemen/

"History of the Middle East." *Wikipedia,* https://en.wikipedia.org/wiki/History_of_the_Middle_East

Hodge, Bodie. "Josephus and Genesis Chapter Ten A Wonderful Stepping-Stone. *Answers in Genesis,* November 18, 2009, https://answersingenesis.org/genesis/josephus-and-genesis-chapter-ten/

"Iran in the Bible." *Farsi Net,* http://www.farsinet.com/iranbibl/

Josephus, Flavius, *The Antiquities of the Jews.* (William Whiston, Trans.) "Chapter 6 How Every Nation Was Denominated From Their First Inhabitants." *Project Gutenberg,* January 4, 2009, https://www.gutenberg.org/files/2848/2848-h/2848-h.htm#link2HCH0006
EBook #2848.

Mark, Joshua J. "The Candaces of Meroe."*Ancient History Encyclopedia*, March 19 2018, https://www.ancient.eu/The_Candaces_of_Meroe/
Mark, Joshua J. "Ur." *Ancient History Encyclopedia*, April 28, 2011, https://www.ancient.eu/ur/

Milstein, Mati. "Petra." *National Geographic,* https://www.nationalgeographic.com archaeology-and-history/archaeology/lost-city-petra/

Mowczko, Marg. "Queen Candace Of Ethiopia." *Ancient History Encyclopedia*, January 24, 2015, https://margmowczko.com/queen-candace-of-the-ethiopians/

"Mt. Nebo." *Tourist Israel,* https://www.touristisrael.com/mount-nebo/16954/

"Old Testament Places Turkey." *Biblical Tour Guide*, https://www.biblicaltourguide.com/oldtestamentplacesturkey.html

"The 12 Tribes Of Ishmael And Their Land." *Jewish Roots of Christianity*, November 6, 2015, http://www.jewishrootsofchristianity.ca/the-12-tribes-of-ishmael-and-their-land/

"Ur of the Chaldees." *Bible History Online*, https://www.bible-history.com/geography/ur_of_chaldees.html

Wood, Bryant G. "Great Discoveries in Biblical Archaeology: The Nuzi Tablets." *Bible and Spade Winter 2005, Associates for Biblical Research,* Posted February 27, 2006, http://www.biblearchaeology.org/post/2006/02/27/Great-Discoveries-in-Biblical-Archaeology-The-Nuzi-Tablets.aspx#Article

Chapter 2 Israel

Ashton, John and David Down. *Unwrapping the Pharoahs : How Egyptian Archaeology Confirms the Biblical Timeline.* Master Books, 2006. Print.

Associated Press. "Jewish global population approaches pre-Holocaust levels." *The Guardian,* June 28, 2015, https://www.theguardian.com/world/2015/jun/28/jewish-global-population-approaches-pre-holocaust-levels

Brown, Shelby. *Late Carthaginian Child Sacrifice and Sacrificial Monuments in Their Mediterranean Context.* UK: Sheffield Academic Press, 1992.

"Dome of the Rock." *Bible Places,* http://www.bibleplaces.com/domeofrock

"Dome of the Rock." *Bible Study Tools*, https://www.biblestudytools.com/commentaries/revelation/related-topics/dome-of-the-rock.html

"Dome of the Rock Shrine, Jerusalem." *Encyclopaedia Britannica*, https://www.britannica.com/topic/Dome-of-the-Rock

Farah, Joseph. "Myths of the Middle East." *World Net Daily,* 2000, http://www.eretzy-israel.org/~jkatz/myths.html

"History of Instant Messaging." *The University of Texas at Austin, Graduate School of Library and Information Science,* https://www.ischool.utexas.edu/~lis312qs/restrict/im/im1.html

"Made in Israel." *CBN,* https://www.youtube.com/watch?v=maMSb8ZIHVE

"Messianic Jews: A Brief History." *Jews for Jesus,* https://jewsforjesus.org/jewish-resources/community/messianic-jews-a-brief-history/

Perlroth, Nicole and Scott Shane. "How Israel Caught Russian Hackers Scouring the World for U.S. Secrets." *The New York Times,* Oct. 10, 2017, https://www.nytimes.com/2017/10/10/technology/kaspersky-lab-israel-russia-hacking.html

"Ur of the Chaldees." *Bible History Online,* https://www.bible-history.com/geography/ur_of_chaldees.html

Versluis, Arie. *The Command to Exterminate the Canaanites: Deuteronomy 7* Leiden|Boston: Brill, 2017.

Wilford, John Noble. "At Ur, Ritual Deaths That Were Anything but Serene." *The New York Times,* October 26, 2009, https://www.nytimes.com/2009/10/27/science/27u.html

Chapter 3 Palestine

"9,000 Photos from 1800's British Mandate of Palestine – with no trace of 'Palestinians'" *The Palestine-Israel Conflict,* February 13, 2013, https://palestineisraelconflict.wordpress.com/2013/02/13/9000-photographs-and-israel-from-1800s-with-no-trace-of-displaced-palestinians/

"Abdullāh I King of Jordan." *Encyclopaedia Britannica,* https://www.britannica.com/biography/Abdullah-I

Alster, Paul. "'Stab the Zionist': Palestinian songs celebrate killing Jews." *Fox News* November 12, 2015, http://www.foxnews.com/world/2015/11/12/sick-hit-parade-palestinian-songs-celebrate-stabbing-jews.html

Aumann, Moshe. *Land Ownership in Palestine, 1880-1948*. Israel Academic Committee on the Middle East (1976)

Balfour, Arthur James. "Balfour Declaration." *Balfour Declaration: Text of the Declaration (November 2, 1917) Jewish Virtual Library*, http://www.jewishvirtuallibrary.org/text-of-the-balfour-declaration

Bard, Mitchell. "West Bank Security Fence: Background & Overview." *Jewish Virtual Library*, http://www.jewishvirtuallibrary.org/background-and-overview-of-israel-s-security-fence

"Black September." *Wikipedia*, https://en.wikipedia.org/wiki/Black_September

"City of David denouncing UNESCO's claims." *The Jerusalem Watch,* March 11, 2018, https://www.youtube.com/watch?v=AIwqnknrH2E

"Demographic History of Palestine." *Wikipedia*, https://en.wikipedia.org/wiki/Demographic_history_of_Palestine_(region)

Farah, Joseph. "Myths of the Middle East." *World Net Daily*, October 11, 2000, http://www.wnd.com/files/2016/09/Joseph-Farah_avatar.jpg

Friedman, Thomas. "Assad Banishes Arafat, And Perhaps Some P.L.O. Hopes." *New York Times*, June 26, 1983, https://www.nytimes.com/1983/06/26/weekinreview/assad-banishes-arafat-and-perhaps-some-plo-hopes.html?mcubz=1

Hattey, Ella. "Palestinians protest new segregation fence in Hebron." *Mondoweiss*, August 29, 2017, http://mondoweiss.net/2017/08/palestinians-protest-segregation/

"Jaffa Colony." https://www.jaffacolony.com/

"Jordanian Annexation of the West Bank." *Wikipedia*, https://en.wikipedia.org/wiki/Jordanian_annexation_of_the_West_Bank

Lazaroff, Tovah. "Israel Declares Hebron and Official Jewish Settlement." *The Jerusalem Post,* August 29, 2017, https://www.jpost.com/Israel-News/Israel-declares-Hebron-an-official-Jewish-settlement-503705

Lovgren, Stefan. "Jerusalem Strife Echoes Ancient History." *National Geographic News,* October 29, 2004, https://news.nationalgeographic.com/news/2004/10/1028_041028_jerusalem_conflict_2.html

"Muhammad in Mecca." *Wikipedia,* https://en.wikipedia.org/wiki/Muhammad_in_Mecca

"Muslim-Western Tensions Persist Common Concerns About Islamic Extremism." *Pew Research Center,* July 21, 2011, http://www.pewglobal.org/2011/07/21/muslim-western-tensions-persist/

Peel, Earl and others. "League of Nations Mandates Palestine Report of the Palestine Royal Commission." *British Palestine Mandate: Text of the Peel Commission Report (July 1937) Jewish Virtual Library,* http://www.jewishvirtuallibrary.org/text-of-the-peel-commission-report

Rogers, James. "DNA discovery identifies living descendants of Biblical Canaanites." *Fox News,* August 1st, 2017, http://www.foxnews.com/science/2017/08/01/dna-discovery-identifies-living-descendants-biblical-canaanites.html

"The Six-Day War: Background & Overview (June 5-10, 1967)." *Jewish Virtual Library,* http://www.jewishvirtuallibrary.org/background-and-overview-six-day-war

Twain, Mark. *The Innocents Abroad.* Hartford, Connecticut: American Publishing Company, 1869. (Gutenberg Press free download.) https://www.gutenberg.org/files/3176/3176-h/3176-h.htm

Wishon, Jennifer. "No More Pay-to-Slay: Will Senate Finally Put an End to PA's Martyr Payments to Terrorists." *CBN News,* February 23, 2018, http://www1.cbn.com/cbnnews/israel/2018/february/no-more-pay-to-slay-will-senate-finally-put-an-end-to-pas-martyr-payments-to-terrorists

Chapter 4 Islamic Terrorism

"Al-Lāt Arabian Deity." *Encyclopaedia Britannica,* https://www.britannica.com/topic/al-Lat

"An Evening with Brigitte Gabriel."*Northwest Liberty News, YouTube,* October 3, 2014, https://www.youtube.com/watch?v=LhC6AxxKIww

"Arab Spring." *Wikipedia,* https://en.wikipedia.org/wiki/Arab_Spring

Bard, Mitchell G. "Lebanon: The History of Modern Lebanon." *Jewish Virtual Library,* http://www.jewishvirtuallibrary.org/the-history-of-modern-lebanon

"Black Stone of Mecca." *Encyclopaedia Britannica,* https://www.britannica.com/topic/Black-Stone-of-Mecca

Di Stefano, Mark. "This Muslim Politician Nailed Why The 'Islam Is Not A Race' Argument Doesn't Work." *Buzz Feed,* April 1, 2017, https://www.buzzfeed.com/markdistefano/aly-on-islam?utm_term=.hi6ldOro2#.purL2ZBWb

Holden, Michael. "Teacher tried to create 'army of children' to launch terror attacks in London," *Reuters,* March 2, 2018. https://www.reuters.com/article/us-britain-security/teacher-tried-to-create-army-of-children-to-launch-terror-attacks-in-london-idUSKCN1GE2CU

"Inside Iran: Signs of the Apocalypse." *CBN News,* http://www1.cbn.com/content/inside-iran-signs-apocalypse

Kabbani, Shaykh Muhammad Hisham (Chairman, Islamic Supreme Council of America) and Shaykh Seraj Hendricks (Head Mufti, Cape Town, South Africa) "Jihad: A Misunderstood Concept from Islam - What Jihad is, and is not." (pg 10) *Islamic Supreme Council,* http://islamicsupremecouncil.org/understanding-islam/legal-rulings/5-jihad-a-misunderstood-concept-from-islam.html?start=9

Maza, Cristina. "ISIS and Al-Qaeda Terrorists Increase Attacks On Western Targets In Africa, Report Reveals." *Newsweek,* February 26, 2018, http://www.newsweek.com/isis-and-al-qaeda-terrorists-increase-attacks-western-targets-jihadist-war-820280

McCarthy, Niall. "The Global Economic Impact Of Terrorism Business #Economy." *Forbes*, November 16, 2017 https://www.forbes.com/sites/niallmccarthy/2017/11/16/the-global-economic-impact-of-terrorism-infographic/#229e44971d0f

Monaghan, Patricia, PhD. "Eastern Mediterranean Pantheon." (pg 30-31) *Encyclopedia of Goddesses and Heroines* https://books.google.com/books?id=Cj5OAwAAQBA&pg=PA30#v=onepage&q&f=false

"Muhammad the Prophet." *History Channel* https://www.youtube.com/watch?v=7w4TH-giaps

Nasser, Riad M. *Palestinian Identity in Jordan and Israel* (pg 100)

Peterson, Daniel C. *Muhammad, Prophet of God.* Grand Rapids:Eerdmans Publishing Co., 2007.

Qur'an Verses.[5.51] O you who believe! do not take the Jews and the Christians for friends; they are friends of each other; and whoever amongst you takes them for a friend, then surely he is one of them; surely Allah does not guide the unjust people [5:57] O you who believe! do not take for guardians those who take your religion for a mockery and a joke, from among those who were given the Book before you and the unbelievers; and be careful of (your duty to) Allah if you are believers. [5.59] Say: O followers of the Book! do you find fault with us (for aught) except that we believe in Allah and in what has been revealed to us and what was revealed before, and that most of you are transgressors? [5.60] Say: Shall I inform you of (him who is) worse than this in retribution from Allah? (Worse is he) whom Allah has cursed and brought His wrath upon, and of whom He made apes and swine, and he who served the Shaitan; these are worse in place and more erring from the straight path.

Shoemaker, Stephan J. *The Death of a Prophet: The End of Muhammad's Life and the Beginnings of Islam.* Philadelphia: University of Pennsylvania Press, 2011.

Sinai, Nicolai and William Montgomery Watt. "Muhammad Prophet Of Islam." *Encyclopaedia Britannica*, April 26, 2018 https://www.britannica.com/biography/Muhammad

Strand, Paul. "Rise of the Mahdi: The Antichrist Poised to Enter World Stage?" *CBN News,* March 3, 2016, http://www1.cbn.com/cbnnews/world/2016/February/Rise-of-the-Mahdi-Why-the-Stage-May-Be-Set-for-the-Antichrist

"The Arab Spring: Five Years On." *Amnesty International,* https://www.amnesty.org/en/latest/campaigns/2016/01/arab-spring-five-years-on/

"The Ottoman Empire." *History,* https://www.history.com/topics/ottoman-empire

"The Ottomans." http://www.theottomans.org/english/history/turkish.asp

"The World's Muslims: Religion, Politics, and Society," *Pew ResearchCenter,* April 30, 2013, http://www.pewforum.org/2013/04/30/the-worlds-muslims-religion-politics-society-overview/

Ward, Clarissa. "In Detail: Sunnis vs. Shiites." *CBS News*, April 5, 2015, https://www.cbsnews.com/news/in-detail-sunnis-vs-shiites/

Wood, David. "Historical Muhammad: The Good, Bad, Downright Ugly." *North American Mission Board,* https://www.namb.net/apologetics/historical-muhammad-the-good-bad-downright-ugly

Wood, David. "Three Stages of Jihad." *YouTube,* https://www.youtube.com/watch?v=ERou_Q5l9Gw

Chapter 5 Bible Prophecies About The Middle East

"Armenian Genocide." *History,* https://www.history.com/topics/armenian-genocide

Baier, Bret. "Study: 90,000 Christians Were Killed for Their Faith in 2016." *Fox News*, Jan.12, 2017, http://insider.foxnews.com/2017/01/12/study-christianity-persecuted-around-world-90k-martyred-2016

Barrow, Tzippe. "Erdogan's Vision: Uniting an 'Army of Islam' to Destroy Israel in 10 Days." *CBN News,* March 13, 2018, http://www1.cbn.com/cbnnews/israel/2018/march/erdogans-vision-army-of-islam-to-destroy-israel

Berkowitz, Adam Eliyahu. "Biblical Origins of the 70-Nation Anti-Israel Paris Conference." *Breaking Israel News,* January 5, 2017, https://www.breakingisraelnews.com/81577/return-70-nations-paris-condemn-israel/#gYhhHPO3yMmF5hs4.97

"Bible prophecies fulfilled by Israel during ancient times." *100 Prophecies,* http://www.100prophecies.org/page5.htm

"Biggest Indian Reservation in the United States." *World Atlas,* https://www.worldatlas.com/articles/biggest-indian-reservations-in-the-united-states.html
https://www.bia.gov/frequently-asked-questions

"Boundaries Of The Land Of Israel—As Set By God." *Jewish Roots of Christianity,* December 25, 2016, http://www.jewishrootsofchristianity.ca/boundaries-of-the-land-of-israel-as-set-by-god/

Brodsky, Matthew RJ. "Is Obama's Hanukkah Gift a Palestinian State?" *The Huffington Post,* December 26, 2016. http://www.matthewrjbrodsky.com/19510/is-obama-hanukkah-gift-a-palestinian-state

Chiaramonte, Perry. "Christians most persecuted group in the world as vicious attacks grow," *Fox News,* April 14, 2017 http://www.foxnews.com/world/2017/04/14/christians-most-persecuted-group-in-world-as-vicious-attacks-grow.html

ChristianPost.com "Thousands of Muslims reportedly turning to Christ in Middle East." *Fox News,* January 11, 2017, http://www.foxnews.com/world/2017/01/11/thousands-muslims-reportedly-turning-to-christ-in-middle-east.html

Connor, Phillip. "Conflicts in Syria, Iraq and Yemen lead to millions of displaced migrants in the Middle East since 2005." *Pew Research Center,* http://www.pewglobal.org/2016/10/18/conflicts-in-syria-iraq-and-yemen-lead-to-millions-of-displaced-migrants-in-the-middle-east-since-2005/

Criss, David and Carma Hassan. "Anti-Semitic incidents rose a whopping 86% in the first 3 months of 2017." *CNN,* April 24, 2017, https://www.cnn.com/2017/04/24/us/antisemitic-incidents-reports-trnd/index.html

Danforth, Nick. "Reclaiming the Ottoman Empire." *Foreign Policy*, October 23, 2016, http://foreignpolicy.com/2016/10/23/turkeys-religious-nationalists-want-ottoman-borders-iraq-erdogan/

David, Ariel. "Before Islam: When Saudi Arabia Was a Jewish Kingdom." *Haaretz*, November 29, 2017, https://www.haaretz.com/archaeology/.premium-before-islam-when-saudi-arabia-was-a-jewish-kingdom-1.5626227

Dearden, Lizzie. *The Independent* "Anti-Semitic attacks hit record high in UK amid warnings over rise of hatred and anger' " *The Independent*, July 26, 2017, https://www.independent.co.uk/news/uk/home-news/anti-semitic-hate-crime-attacks-british-jews-assaults-uk-incidents-record-high-cst-research-a7861721.html

Estrin, Daniel. "Debate over Jewish prayer at Temple Mount heats up," *The Times of Israel*, December 18, 2013 https://www.timesofisrael.com/debate-over-jewish-prayer-at-temple-mount-heats-up/

"Ezekiel's Plates." *Biblical Archaeology Truth*, http://www.biblicalarchaeologytruth.com/ezekiels-plates.html

"Groundhog Day Forecasts and Climate History." *National Centers for Environmental Information* https://www.ncei.noaa.gov/news/groundhog-day-forecasts-and-climate-history

Hasson, Nir. "Jewish Activists to Reenact Passover Sacrifice at Foot of Temple Mount." *Haaretz*, March 26, 2018, https://www.haaretz.com/israel-news/.premium-jerusalem-police-authorize-passover-sacrifice-at-foot-of-temple-mount-1.5939769

Hasson, Nir. "Temple Mount Activists Plan Passover Sacrifice Near Western Wall." *Haaretz*, March 29, 2017, https://www.haaretz.com/israel-news/.premium-temple-mount-activists-plan-passover-sacrifice-near-western-wall-1.5454562

"How Would the Accuracy of Biblical Prophets Compare to Today's Psychics?" *Y-Jesus*, https://y-jesus.com/how-would-the-accuracy-of-biblical-prophets-compare-to-todays-psychics/

"ISIS Egypt affiliate: Christians are our "favorite prey.'" *Fox News,* February 20, 2017, http://www1.cbn.com/cbnnews/israel/2018/march/erdogans-vision-army-of-islam-to-destroy-israel

Issaev, Leonid. "Can Russia, Iran and Turkey agree on a roadmap for Syria?" *Al Jazeera,* April 5, 2018, https://www.aljazeera.com/indepth/opinion/russia-iran-turkey-agree-roadmap-syria-180405111004526.html

Janelle P in Middle East. Muslims Turn To Christ In Unprecedented Numbers PT 1." *Open Doors,* June 28, 2017, https://www.opendoorsusa.org/christian-persecution-stories/muslims-turn-to-christ-in-unprecedented-numbers-pt-1/

Khoury, Jack. "From the West Bank to London The Palestinian Plan to Protest the Balfour Declaration's 100th Anniversary." *Haaretz,* October 26, 2017, https://www.haaretz.com/middle-east-news/palestinians/.premium-the-palestinian-plan-to-protest-the-balfour-declaration-s-100th-anniversary-1.5460456

Lefkovits, Etgar. "Road To Temple Mount Uncovered." *Jerusalem Post,* March 31 2006, https://www.jpost.com/Israel/Road-to-Temple-Mount-uncovered

Mitchell, Chris. "Prophecy Fulfilled: City of David 'Shakes Off the Dust.'" *CBN News,* August 14, 2017, http://www1.cbn.com/cbnnews/israel/2017/march/prophecy-fulfilled-city-of-david-shakes-off-the-dust

Mora, Edwin. "Expert: Erdogan Regime Considers Christians, Jews 'Enemies of the State.'" *Breitbart,* March 12, 2018, http://www.breitbart.com/national-security/2018/03/12/expert-erdogan-regime-considers-christians-jews-enemies-of-state/

"Nablus (Shechem)." *Jewish Virtual Library,* http://www.jewishvirtuallibrary.org/nablus-shechem

Nikbakht, Daniel and Sheena McKenzie. "The Yemen war is the world's worst humanitarian crisis, UN says." *CNN,* April 3, 2018, https://www.cnn.com/2018/04/03/middleeast/yemen-worlds-worst-humanitarian-crisis-un-intl/index.html

Pongratz-Lippitt, Christa. "Europe's disregard for Christian persecution 'almost sinister.'" *The Tablet,* February 6, 2018, http://www.thetablet.co.uk/news/8523/europe-s-disregard-for-christian-persecution-almost-sinister-

"Push To Rebuild Jerusalem Temple Has Earth-Shaking Implications." *World Net Daily,* April 17,2017, http://www.wnd.com/2017/04/push-to-rebuild-jerusalem-temple-has-earth-shaking-implications/

Rollins, Adrian and David Walker. "How accurate are economic forecasts?" *In The Black,* April 1, 2016, https://www.intheblack.com/articles/2016/04/01/how-accurate-are-economic-forecasts

Robertson, Gordon. "The Seat of Satan: Nazi Germany." *CBN News,* http://www1.cbn.com/700club/seat-satan-nazi-germany

Rudee, Eliana. "5 Biblical Prophecies Fulfilled in 2017 and 5 More Expected in 2018." *Breaking Israel News,* January 5, 2018 https://www.breakingisraelnews.com/100479/5-biblical-prophecies-fulfilled-2017-5-expected-2018/#/

Schemm, Paul. "ISIS destroys ancient artifacts in Iraq as a cover for an even more sinister activity." *Business Insider,* May. 12, 2015, http://www.businessinsider.com/isis-destroys-ancient-artifacts-in-iraq-as-a-cover-for-an-even-more-sinister-activity-2015-5

Shamoun, Sam. "Responses to Islamic Awareness Christian Analysis of the Islamic Awareness' Alleged Rebuttal to: Prophet Muhammad's Night Journey To Al-Masjid Al-Aqsâ - The Farthest Mosque."http://www.answering-islam.org/Responses/Saifullah/aqsa.htm

Stoner, Peter W., M.S. and Robert C. Newman, S.T.M., Ph.D.*Science Speaks.* (Chapter 3 "The Christ of Prophecy.") Chicago: Moody Press, Revised 2005. Online book, http://sciencespeaks.dstoner.net/

"Ten Bible prophecies fulfilled recently." *The Refiners Fire,* https://www.therefinersfire.org/recent_prophecy.htm

The City of David." *Jewish Virtual Library,* http://www.jewishvirtuallibrary.org/the-city-of-david

"The Making of Transjordan." http://www.kinghussein.gov.jo/his_transjordan.html

Volkmann, Hans. "Antiochus-IV-Epiphanes." *Encyclopaedia Britannica,* https://www.britannica.com/biography/Antiochus-IV-Epiphanes

Weber, Jeremy. " 'Worst Year Yet': The Top 50 Countries Where It's Hardest to Be a Christian." *Christianity Today,* January 11, 2017, https://www.christianitytoday.com/news/2017/january/top-50-countries-christian-persecution-world-watch-list.html

"Who Has A Legal Right to the Land?" *Fruits of Zion,* June 14 ,2016, https://ffoz.org/discover/israel-history/who-has-a-legal-right-to-the-land.html

www.ingramcontent.com/pod-product-compliance
Lightning Source LLC
Chambersburg PA
CBHW051952290426
44110CB00015B/2211